THE BORDER AND THE LINE

Stanford Studies in
COMPARATIVE RACE AND ETHNICITY

THE BORDER
AND THE LINE

Race, Literature, and Los Angeles

Dean J. Franco

Stanford University Press
Stanford, California

Stanford University Press

Stanford, California

Printed in the United States of America on acid-free, archival-quality paper

Library of Congress Cataloging-in-Publication Data available upon request.

Designed by Kevin Barrett Kane

Typeset by Kevin Barrett Kane in 10.5/15 Adobe Garamond

Cover design by Rob Ehle

To Ari and Gabriel

CONTENTS

ACKNOWLEDGMENTS

It's an understatement to say that I began this project after I read Helena María Viramontes's novel *Their Dogs Came with Them*, a book that affected me so profoundly that I put it down and decided not to write about it at all until I came to a broader understanding of the ethics and politics of place adequate to Viramontes's achievement. Over the years, many people helped me get there, beginning with Helena herself, first when she visited with me and my students at Wake Forest, and later when I visited with her at Cornell University, where Liz Anker invited me to speak. The general conception of the book accelerated during that visit, especially as a result of some great conversations with Caroline Levine, Mary Pat Brady, and Dagmawi Woubshet. I am especially grateful to Liz for giving me a key suggestion about metaphor that substantiated my book (yet again!). Sarah Imhoff convened a roundtable discussion on new directions in Jewish studies at Indiana University, where I presented the earliest version of my thoughts on the L.A. Eruv; Bruce Barnhart invited me to participate in a conference at the University of Oslo, where I ventured sections of my chapter on

Budd Schulberg and Paul Beatty; and Benjamin Schreier hosted me at
Penn State for a lecture on the Watts Writers Workshop. I am grateful
to Liz, Sarah, Bruce, and Ben, and their respective institutions and
audiences for their support of this project. I offer my thanks, too, to
Leonardo Vilchis, whose work with *Union de Vecinos* in Los Angeles
is the subject of the final section of the first chapter. Over multiple
visits, Leonardo guided me through the work of *Union de Vecinos* in
East L.A., introduced me to local neighbors, and fed my habit for
breakfast tamales. I offer thanks to Donna Myrow, journalist, edu-
cator, and amanuensis for the Watts Writers Workshop, for sharing
memories and insights about Budd Schulberg. Finally, while dwelling
on California, I offer thanks to Paula Moya, who received my initial
queries about this book with warmth and steadily encouraged me as
I wrote—such a model of professional graciousness.

Closer to home, my colleagues at Wake Forest University are ceaselessly generous and encouraging, and constitute a lively, intellectually
engaged community in which to write a book. Matt Garite gave me
expert advice on how to think about the Watts riots in relation to
labor, and Jarrod Whitaker, Omaar Hena, Jessica Richard, Herman
Rapaport, Susan Harlan, Chris Brown, and Mary Foskett read or en-
dured half-baked drafts and ideas so you didn't have to. Colleagues at
the Wake Forest School of Law invited me to speak on the ethics and
politics of the neighbor while I was drafting the third chapter, helping
me hone my thinking. My research and writing has been supported by
Wake Forest with a generous Reynolds Leave, and funding for summer travel to Dartmouth College's Rauner Special Collections Library
from the Wake Forest Archie fund.

If Viramontes's novel made me want to write a book that felt
true to the complexities of place, my wider community of friends has
helped me understand the lived experience of neighborliness. Ken Put-
nam and Matt Canter are among the first locals I met when I moved
to Winston-Salem over a decade ago and I walked into Ken's Bike
Shop, and they help constitute a neighborhood in the best way—open,

resourceful, caring. Over the course of countless rides and hundreds of miles on our bicycles, Tony McGee and Sean Barb taught me about the tactics of counter-cartography common to both neighborhood organizers in Los Angeles and insurgent North Carolina trail builders. Nicole Whitaker shared her enthusiasm and interest in geography, as I tried out my early-stage ideas, and Adrienne Pilon—once again—read everything here, offering comment, critique, and a shared love of people and places in Los Angeles. I am grateful to Adrienne's partnership as we traversed L.A. at large and Boyle Heights in particular, and for our sons who came along, with growing intellectual and creative interest over the years. Those sons, Ari and Gabriel, made me want to write a book that might matter. This book is dedicated to them.

THE BORDER AND THE LINE

THE BORDERS AND LINES
OF SOCIAL IDENTITIES

PICO BOULEVARD IN Los Angeles runs mostly west-east, from Santa Monica near the ocean shore into downtown Los Angeles, a transect which reveals the overlap of communities that constitute greater L.A. Crossing the 10, 405, and 110 freeways, Pico is itself an off-ramp on a journey to and from somewhere else. Pico's distinct neighborhoods, its segmentation, and its length mean that people don't typically drive it end to end. Rather, they take it on in parts. Thus a transect of L.A. along Pico is a study in the city's economic, linguistic, ethnic, sonic, and culinary diversity, as one neighborhood abruptly if unceremoniously gives way to another. Driving along Pico with the windows rolled down, you are bound to hear rap, reggae, cumbia, and Cambodian psyche-rock. And you may see or perhaps even smell signs of Mexican, Central American, and East Asian cooking along the way. Here is how food writer Jonathan Gold puts it:

The street plays host to the unglamorous bits of Los Angeles, the row of one-stops that supply records to local jukeboxes, the kosher-pizza district, the auto-body shops that speckle its length the way giant churches speckle

Wilshire. And while Pico may divide neighborhoods more than it creates them—Koreatown from Harvard Heights, Wilshire Center from Midtown, Beverly-Hills-adjacent from not-all-that-Beverly-Hills-adjacent, neighborhoods your cousin Martha lives in from neighborhoods she wouldn't step into after dark—there isn't even a Pico-identified gang.[1]

The cheeky last line about the lack of a gang is in fact an indication of the odd fluidity of Pico, where, for all its discrete segments, there are no neighborhood borders so resolute as to mandate territorial defense.

When I was growing up in the 1970s, Pico Boulevard was the off-ramp my parents took coming up from Orange County to visit my mother's parents, who lived in the Pico-Robertson district. My grandparents purchased that home in the 1960s after living all over Los Angeles, from downtown to Boyle Heights and MacArthur Park (my mother's childhood homes) and finally to Beverlywood. Pico-Robertson is now famously "Jewish L.A.," but it wasn't when my grandparents moved there, and it's doubtful that that distinction would have held any attraction for them. My grandfather was a Sephardic Jew from Turkey and my grandmother a Catholic immigrant from El Salvador, though neither was religious, and my grandfather maintained a fury toward religion that strikes me only now as typical of Jewish atheists. I am told that each was treated as something of a pariah by family after the intermarriage, but the upshot is that I didn't grow up knowing my relatives, and only discovered that my grandmother's sisters all lived in greater L.A. when she died and a collection of light-brown-skinned women arrived at her funeral, speaking Spanish and pressing my cheeks with their lips, soft in exactly the way my grandmother's lips were.

So Pico, the freeway exit, is indelibly linked with a strangeness I only later came to associate with ethnic difference. These women were my ostensible connection to Hispanic Los Angeles, and later in graduate school when I told a faculty mentor I was Sephardic, I learned that Pico-Robertson is home to many Sephardic Jews. Typically, this would be the place in this Introduction to display my authentic, genetic, identitarian credentials, my authority to write this book. But I feel no such authority, and I have no claims to make, other than to say that race and ethnicity are material and experiential phenomena, meted out locally, even if promulgated, stabilized, and circulated through national and global forces. If my family's identity grants me any authority it is perhaps a claim on curiosity and a commitment to understanding the strange ways in which identities can be two things at once, signs of access and signs of constraint. I always felt like an outsider to L.A., and I suspect my grandparents often did, too. My mother certainly did, though she grew up there—she wasn't a member of the Jewish community and certainly not of the Hispanic community. This is a book deeply suspicious of claims of authenticity, and I offer up neither my own nor anyone else's identity as a stand-in for some broader claim about ethnicity. Rather, my chief argument in this book is that social identities such as race and ethnicity are localized, contingent accruals of discrete experience in time and space, and though we necessarily use broad terms such as *Hispanic*, *Jewish*, and *African American* precisely for their diachronic capacity—that is, the way they connect people across time—we nonetheless experience our social identities immediately, in a given moment, at a given time and place. Like Pico Boulevard, our social identities are a series of segments that run into each other inelegantly, and if I may extend the metaphor, we access them like we exit a freeway: all of a sudden immersion in a world of difference that is deeply felt if highly contingent. And like freeways, they are also socially and politically produced, often state-sponsored if also state failures.

The Border and the Line is about the spatial materialization of racial identity, and it looks to three neighborhoods in Los Angeles for case studies of how to think about what race is and to explore the ethics and politics of interracial engagements. My study and critique of racial formation in and across boundaries is not about racial materialism versus post-racialism, not about race versus ethnicity, nor a celebration of intersectionality (though celebrate it I do). Nor is this book about locality versus globality (and certainly not about the dreaded "glocal") as a study of the location of cultures. Race exists; it has a material, discursive, and psychical reality. Michael Omi and Howard Winant's coinage of the term *racial formation* aptly captures the way race is formed at simultaneously different scales: "At the micro-level, race is a matter of individuality, of the formation of *identity*. . . . At the macro-level, race is a matter of *collectivity*, of the formation of social structures."[2] Omi and Winant are primarily interested in state-based collective racialization, though this present book seeks to intertwine the two modes of racial formation because even as race materializes through racist practices, race remains a resource of self-awareness and communal consciousness. Race comprises intersections of identities, certainly, but it also materializes *at* intersections, as subjects move though space. As Gaye Theresa Johnson among others has observed, across the twentieth century, minority communities in Los Angeles were "scattered" by city planners in order to maintain "the hegemony of business owners and their efforts to maintain LA as an open-shop city."[3] Racial capitalism's marginalization of minorities materializes racial difference as political powerlessness, yet the cultural production of racial minorities, through music, food, and alternative forms and uses of transportation, constitutes what Johnson calls "spatial entitlement," or the envisioning of new identities and affiliations among minority populations (1).[4] How that works—how race can be simultaneously pernicious and affirming, and how racial boundary crossing can undermine or substantiate racial community—that is the subject of this book.

In *The Border and the Line* I argue for cross-racial analysis and develop a method for reconciling discursive and materialist accounts of race and ethnicity as the basis of future comparative work. I compare the identities of specific neighborhoods in Los Angeles through an examination of the production of space in East and West L.A.; through conversations with community organizers and religious practitioners; and through analyses of literature by Helena María Viramontes, Paul

Beatty, Budd Schulberg, James Baldwin, and the writers of the Watts
Writers Workshop (1965–1973).[5] Los Angeles is the object for my study
of the ethics and politics of the neighbor because its neighborhoods are
at once protean and concrete. Since the 1960s, the racial demographics
of any given neighborhood have shifted restlessly, with white flight to
the Westside and the Valley, the increase of Latinos in South Central,
and the growth of the black middle class in central west L.A. At the
same time, property and political values in Los Angeles produce and
depend on insiders and outsiders, the elite and the abject, sustained
by the spatial and material production of race, a process that yields
perennial economic inequality among regions of Los Angeles and static
life options for the poorest.[6]

By studying the spatial and material construction of race in Los
Angeles, I bring together different accounts of what race is and how
it works, and forecast new kinds of cross-racial encounters in literature and in the world around. Especially in the humanities, race is
often regarded as the effect of language, invented and sustained by
discourse. In this regard, race is a phantasm, something we perpetuate by talking about it, and something we strive to reduce through
ostensibly progressive "post-racial" critique.[7] This view locates race
amid controlling regimes of "biopolitics," the management of categories of persons as part of the larger project of the state's control
of life and death options for its subjects. This discursive approach to
race contrasts the other prevailing approach, which considers race as
a material effect: enslavement and colonialism, immigration quotas,
Jim Crow laws, redlining practices, quasi-legal domination—all are
the material means by which race is inscribed upon the body, and by
which the bodies of those racialized constitute a given race.[8] Across
three substantial chapters, *The Border and the Line* explores a meeting
point between these two modes of thinking about race, the discursive
and material, as it stages analyses across racial and ethnic groups. This
book is fundamentally comparative, and in the Conclusion, as in the
conclusions to my prior two books, I make the case for comparative

race studies as an indispensable methodology for understanding just what race is and how it works. Here, however, the individual chapters are not comparative per se. Rather, each is a deep-dive into a neighborhood, a narrative, and a racial formation that surpasses the starting concept—a racial name, or a neighborhood characteristic, say—on the way to understanding how the borders and lines of a given place materialize social identity. Across the three chapters, I demonstrate that borders function in vastly different ways for different people in different locales, at different times. This means I cannot sum up a single analytic or thesis about the spatial materialization of race, and it means that no one chapter captures a fundamental, summary logic of identity. Rather, what should become clear to a reader of this book is that racial formation and racial recognition function asymmetrically for different people depending on the material circumstances of their lives. I have more to say about how to read this differential account further on, but for now I posit that among this book's chief contributions to understanding racialization is the reader's encounter with that difference, and that a reader of this book can expect to continually revisit key scenes and critical topoi, with each pass giving a different angle of understanding, on the way to accumulating a multidimensional account of race and space.

To be a little more specific, Los Angeles is a city of contradictions, and race and other forms of identity are themselves self-contradictory modes of categorization, so I have organized this book in such a way as to dwell in and reveal those contradictions. As but one material example, consider the freeway, the topic of so much L.A. writing and an important critical motif. The freeway connects and divides, simultaneously. The Hollywood Freeway (101), for instance forms the western boundary of Boyle Heights and traces the contours of the prewar, color-coded maps which "redlined" that neighborhood as a racial threat. Redlining depressed housing values and economically cut off the area from the rest of Los Angeles, and the freeway functions in the same way. The construction of these freeways, documented in Helena María

Viramontes's writing, ripped apart neighborhoods. Yet these same free-ways were the passageways for Budd Schulberg's commute to Watts, where he established his writing workshop for indigent writers after the 1965 riots. The Hollywood Freeway serves as one of the boundary walls that effectively shape a "courtyard" for Orthodox Jews living within the Los Angeles Community Eruv, the ritually circumscribed communal space of religious belonging. The forms of constraint and access (the *eruv* achieves both) at work in all three instances requires a deep and extended look into the material, psychological, ethical, and political dimensions of distinct situations of identity formation. In this regard, I do not make extended, head-to-head comparisons of neighborhoods within chapters. Rather, a comparison unfolds through rise or fall of the salience of ethics or politics, metaphor or metonymy, or access or constraint as the dominant mode of boundary formation and border crossing. Chapters continually refer to one another, and key terms, quo-tations, and analytical moves are posited in one place and picked up in another, with the intended effect of mapping Los Angeles's contradic-tory and simultaneous modes of producing racial identities.

This is not a book about Los Angeles per se; no one reading it should expect a comprehensive history or ethnography of the city or the neighborhoods in question. Rather, I reflect on L.A.'s network of boundaries in order to materially and cognitively map the emergence of social identities, and to examine the ethical and political implica-tions of boundary crossing. Doing so will allow a granular view of race and space that otherwise tends to fade when those topics are examined in broader national, hemispheric, and global frameworks. While I do not contest the argument that racialization has a global cast to it—that black-American self-identification drew energy from African decolo-nization across the twentieth century, or that Chicana/o identity was self-aware of a hemispheric politics of *latinidad*, say—I nonetheless maintain that racial identity and especially racial identification have a local dimension.[9] Indeed, identification, or the experience of being raced, maps on to the famous scenario of hegemonic identification, the "hailing" that Louis Althusser describes as the immediate contact with ideological formation when the hegemon points a finger and says "Hey, you!"[10] Notably, in Althusser's scenario the finger-pointer is proximate, perhaps even familiar: we expect him, we know what corner he stands on, and we are not surprised that passing by him resulted in this sort of calling out, as if he marked some kind of unspoken but recognized boundary and crossing him would have the consequence of social and ideological identification.

In this way, I posit that the neighborhood is the geography of racial identification and racial experience. Similarly, María Josefina Saldaña-Portillo argues that "racial geography is a technology of power, and when used as an analytic and theory of spatial production, it indexes the series of techniques used to produce space in racial terms."[11] Saldaña-Portillo's scope is hemispheric and historical, while mine is local and experiential, situated in and figured by the geography of the neighborhood. The word *neighborhood* bears its own gravity, pulling in a series of orbiting virtues we wish to assign to the concept. Neighborhoods are where people care for each other, where petty politics give way to more enduring relations of trust. Neighborhoods are also the sites of privilege, defense, and paranoia, and not only those that are exclusive or gated. As Paul Beatty makes clear in *The Sellout*, poor people of color defend their territory with pride of place as much as wealthy residents of Beverly Hills do.[12] Though I will unpack this point in later chapters, here I posit that the neighborhood is a crossroads of ethics and politics, of individual identity and corporate identification.

The "neighbor" is variously a theological, theoretical, and political construct (in Augustine, Levinas, and Arendt, respectively, to name but three resources).[13] The neighbor is an especially rich figure that can be mobilized to advance an ethics we associate with reading literature—love, recognition, care—into a politics typically associated with activism—responsibility, reparation, and remedy. The neighbor has received substantial theoretical attention in the past decade, but most writing on the neighbor remains philosophical, and rarely if ever addresses real neighbors in real neighborhoods.[14] If the theological or theoretical neighbor is the potential figure for recognition and love, real neighborhoods are more politically tricky, often locations of both inclusion and exclusion, love and fear. In this way, across three chapters I demonstrate that the neighbor is representative of both the divide in approaches to thinking about race and the potential reconciliation of those approaches. Wishing to sustain both the conceptual and material accounts of the neighbor, I pin my analysis on a particular place, Los Angeles, and particular neighborhoods in Los Angeles that are at once racially sequestered and sites of productive instances of interracial crossings. Literature allows us to understand how borders and barriers malfunction, and my cross-racial readings substantiate the efficacy of comparative criticism in ethnic American literature.

LOS ANGELES

A fairly straightforward account of Los Angeles history would begin by observing that Los Angeles was not always such a segregated city. Indeed, upon its founding at the end of the eighteenth century, its population was composed of Mexicans, including indigenous Californians and African-ancestry settlers and landowners. The city remained sleepy through the mid-1800s, though vastly expanded in the latter half of that century with the general westward population migration, drawn by the federal promise of free land and the facilitation of land usurpation from Mexican owners following the end of the Mexican-American War in 1848. That migration was accelerated by the completion of railroad lines at the end of the nineteenth century, and then the purchase of large land tracts by industrialist developers in the early twentieth century. That Pico Boulevard is named after the two-term governor of Alta California before U.S. annexation in 1848 makes an interesting kind of sense. Pío Pico's personal history is embedded in the early history of Southern California.[15] As a landowner, rancher, and developer in the late nineteenth century, Pico battled with the changing legal realities of U.S. annexation, and his losing fight to keep his land was typical of many *Californios*, who lost property to settler-squatters. Pico was born in poverty in San Diego in 1801, at the end of the Spanish reign over Mexico; acquired vast amounts of land over the course of his early life, through land grants and speculation; became the last governor of California under Mexican rule in 1845; and died in poverty in a new California in 1894.[16]

In the two decades after Pico's death, Los Angeles was transformed by the westward migration of settlers, merchants, miners, and land speculators. The influx of Mexicans, Japanese, Chinese, and Jewish laborers in the early twentieth century disturbed white utopian dreams, with white people marshalling overt and institutional white supremacist tactics. Klan activity increased, and white city patriarchs colluded to sequester minorities in undesirable tracts of land.[17] Indeed, L.A.'s famously expansive area facilitated the development of a series of new white enclaves on the city's west and north sides across the twentieth century, while redlining real estate practices and subsequent infrastructure construction effectively sequestered minority-dominant populations in the industrial east and south sections of the city.

But notice how my thumbnail sketch of the city is written in such a way as to naturalize racial difference. Let me put it another, even more straightforward way: from the late nineteenth century to the present, people seeking competitive advantage in Los Angeles secured status through the materialization of race: burning crosses, donning white robes, and, crucially, constructing boundaries through law and building practices that clarified and ramified racial difference. Japanese and Chinese immigrant laborers, African American migrants, and Jewish merchants newly arrived or even long established (especially in the case of Jews) were materially distinguished as racially distinct by these very practices, and whiteness and racial otherness were mutually composed by the city's expansion and restrictions across the early to mid-twentieth century. This is not to say that people didn't already have racial identities, but that those identities became materially significant through a set of practices. Those practices were both figurative, as minorities were recast as racial menace, and material, as white patriarchs channeled city resources to select neighborhoods and shunted resources away from others. Though white people used overt, violent racism as a tool, whiteness had no particular history to conserve in Los Angeles, and so white supremacy became manifest not as a tradition but as a tactic—a mechanism for evading the racial history of the rest of the country, even as white people in L.A. benefitted from the increasing social and cartographical immobility of people of color during the twentieth century.

The concentration of minorities in segregated neighborhoods in the eastern and southern districts of the city, combined with the growth of port-related labor during World War II, as well as manufacturing, domestic labor, and the growth of garment work, meant that minorities who were restricted from buying property outside of redlined districts nonetheless had regular contact with the rest of the city. This is illustrated in Chester Himes's 1945 novel *If He Hollers, Let Him Go*, in which the African American protagonist who lives in San Pedro regularly drives all over Los Angeles, showing up to meet a girlfriend on the mostly white Westside, driving downtown, cruising the Eastside, all the while earning the enmity of locals and the police while responding in kind with his own contempt for the unwritten laws of racial containment.[18] That novel ends with the protagonist locked up over false rape charges, and he is only able to escape imprisonment when he agrees to serve in the military, an ultimate form of containment. Himes's novel illustrates what I will analyze further on, the way boundaries circumscribe and identify people, even and perhaps precisely as they fail to contain them.

Los Angeles's strategies for producing and managing race are not exceptional, but the city's population shifts and flows are indeed unique. No other city in the United States has such a quicksilver character, seems so ahistorical, and is yet so segregated. *The Border and the Line* explains this simultaneous containment and flow, and analyzes the cooperation of lines of division and fluid borders. I am examining literature, film, and, let us say in the vein of Elizabeth Povinelli, "alternative social projects"—that is, ways of living that are unsanctioned and even oppositional to liberalism—in order to explore at some length the mechanisms by which containment and flow occur, and to reflect on and perhaps theorize with the experiences that pertain to living amid those mechanisms.[19] To be clear, then, this is not a sociological account of the racial formation of Jews, African Americans, and Chicanos of Los Angeles, nor is it an attempt to generalize about those groups or groupings of literature at large. I am not trying to say what African American literature set in Los Angeles is "really about," nor am I trying to say something about inter-ethnic Jewishness that would tell us about Jews in general. This is not a book about "in general," in general. Instead, it is about how social-group identification forms in relation to boundaries, where racial assignment is shot through with divisive lines, and about how crossing borders involves a remapping of identity analogous to the remapping of space.[20]

While I am at it, I am not suggesting that certain material features of the neighborhoods of Los Angeles can be metaphorized into a general ethics of neighborliness. Indeed, to the contrary, this is a book written against or at least as an alternative to exemplariness. This is not a manifesto for locality, but it is a demonstration of how the local and immediate configure and stabilize (just before they are destabilized) prevailing notions of race and ethnicity. If anything, I am writing to make the case that race and ethnicity, indeed "race" and "ethnicity," are themselves metaphorical agencies which often block understanding of the more dynamic flux and flow that determines social life. That flux and flow is traceable globally, hemispherically, and transnationally, though with our broadest accounts we must install generalized concepts of groups in order to represent the traffic of people and culture. Examining a very local scene in a fairly bracketed time and place obviates the need to generalize, and gives us a look into what lies beneath those generalities in the first place.

IDENTITY AT THE CROSSROADS
OF METAPHOR AND METONYMY

Though we typically think of ourselves as complexly composed of several identities, with each coming into relevance more or less depending on our situation, we are nonetheless bound by bluntly totalizing terminology that regularly fails to capture the fact of race. At one point in his 2008 campaign for the presidency, Barack Obama had fun with how his own complex story is reduced by racial nomenclature, telling comedian Jon Stewart that since he was "half-black and half-white," he would be at odds with himself in the voting booth (he even went so far as to mime pulling the voting lever with one hand while reaching out to stop himself with the other hand).[21] We laugh, but can we do better? In *Identity Complex*, Michael Hames-García explains the problem this way: "Whereas personal identities and selves contain infinite complexity and variety, social groups—either as political actors or as demographic categories—tend toward a reductive homogeny."[22] Hames-García posits the multiply constituted subject, and argues for a theory of social identities that accounts for multiplicity—multiplicity rather than hybridity or even intersectionality, in which the dynamism of social selves is interactive with the ever variable complexity of social life.

My claims here are allied with Hames-García's, and I add a dimension to his account of multiplicity by asking what happens politically and ethically when one passes in and out of differently identified spaces. A university student of color, for example, may live in a dorm with a variety of other people of color where she has sought community, yet may find herself one of only a few students of color in any given class, a scenario I observe frequently. That same student may visit with her family on break, where she is immersed in a communal identity so homogenous as to obviate (and perhaps relieve her) of identity's constant prod to the psyche. As this student moves among different spaces, the very same identities may dilate or contract in political importance. Hames-García argues that "the subjective experience of any social identity *always* depends fundamentally on relations to other social identities," which suggests not only that our social identity is fluid, but that it shifts and changes as we move through space, especially as we cross through neighborhoods and experience the recession or emergence of this or that aspect of our social identity.[23] Implicit in Hames-García's account of multiplicity, then, is narrative, or the world-making that occurs as a subject moves through time and space, encountering and being changed by difference. Indeed, it can be difficult to disambiguate a rhetoric of racial identity from a rhetoric of racial boundaries, as terms such as *hood*, and *wrong side of the tracks*, and the racial constraint at work in outlawed real estate practices make clear. To say a neighborhood was "redlined" is to note simultaneously its boundaries and its racial character. Obviously, narratives about social identities will necessarily foreground this sort of multiplicity, and telling the story of local movements along and across boundaries likewise suggests how constructs of race become more or less fixed and more or less fluid as people move in and out of neighborhoods.

The interplay between what Hames-García calls the social "homogeny" of group identity and the relationality at work in identity formation is comparable to the signifying function of metaphor and metonymy, a point I will develop at some length in Chapter 1. Hames-García's account is in accord with Paula Moya's "post-positivist" claim that identities are "socially significant and context-specific ideological constructs that nevertheless refer in non-arbitrary (if partial) ways to verifiable aspects of the social world."[24] Returning to the student in the scenario, let's say she's a brown Latina. But what do I mean by "brown Latina"? In some contexts, she may feel called upon to represent her identity (or she may resist just such a call), as when she's the only visibly identifiable Latina in a class that is discussing immigration. In that instance, her identity signifies metaphorically, as if all of the history and culture of a given group of people is carried over and placed upon her back (we recall that "carry over" is the etymological root of "metaphor"). In another context, this same young woman, at home among her family and friends, is embedded in a culture of contingency, where who she is is nothing other than who she is with and what she is doing. Her identity is less a matter of how she is perceived from the outside than it is composed in contingent relation with the group of which she is an insider. Counterintuitively, this may mean that the woman of my example is *less* Latina-identified when among her friends, though if asked to describe what *Latina* means, she may refer to precisely these local experiences. I recall a line from a Philip Roth novel, in which the narrator describes living in an all-Jewish neighborhood—the picnics, the schools, the fathers and sons playing baseball on the weekends—and reflects, "[W]e didn't think about being Jewish. Jewish was just what we were." This is what I will refer to throughout the book as metonymical identity—identity's formation through social location, through apposition and chains of association, and through context and contingency.

If metaphorical identification is embedded in history as a raft of beliefs, practices, or folkways carried over through time, metonymical identity is more synchronic and more spatially determined. I will argue that when we speak about race, we more or less use metaphor and metonymy as the rhetorical forms of racial discourse. "More or less," because identities are either more or less continuous or broken, diachronically holistic or synchronically contingent, though both are usually in play at once, highlighting, as Mary Pat Brady puts it, "the sociality of space and the spatiality of language."[25] Distinctly, the recent return to prominence of *black* over *African American* bears neither transparent history nor geography, and the atavistic genetic connotations speak more to some concept of race than of culture. What *black* signals now—as in "black lives matter"—is the immediate, present-time experience of racialization, wherein the biological atavism of race returns as the material and violent racialization of a body of people made to be black for the purposes of economic exploitation and the maintenance of social boundaries and hierarchies. Writing about Chicago, Rashad Shabazz argues, "[T]he presence of policing, surveillance, restrictions on mobility, and the enforcing of territory had significant impact on the production of Black masculinity."[26] That a form of blackness is not only policed but produced indicates how race is a material, metonymical configuration that appears through the distillation and dispersal of very real social and political forces, both enforced and contested.

African American certainly bears with it metonymical traces of geography, and *black* likewise metaphorically carries over a history of racialization, because though we are typically inclined to sort out metaphor and metonymy, the two rhetorical figures constantly cooperate and bleed into each other, blurring borders of signification. When Barack Obama noted that if he had a son, that boy would look like Trayvon Martin, he was both metaphorically substituting himself for Martin—saying, "Carry over what happened there and it could happen to me or any black man"—and metonymically signaling how blackness is conditioned as vulnerability to police violence.[27]

I take the time to linger on the rhetoric or racial designation because race exists in and as an effect of language, and because language responds to and generates its own material, political reality. The latter is Ernesto Laclau's point in his book on rhetorical forms. First grounding his discussion in twentieth century structuralist linguistics, Laclau posits that "metaphor and metonymy . . . are not just some figures among many, but the two fundamental matrices around which all other figures and tropes should be ordered."[28] Noting that metaphor is fundamentally about substitutability and continuity, and metonymy about contiguity and placement, Laclau concludes,

"Continuity" shades into "analogy," "metonymy" into "metaphor." Anticipating what I will discuss presently, we can see that this is inherent to the central political operation that I call "hegemony": the movement from metonymy to metaphor, from *contingent* articulation to *essential* belonging. The name—of a social movement, of an ideology, of a political institution—is always the metaphorical crystallization of contents whose analogical links result from concealing the contingent contiguity of their metonymical origins. Conversely, the dissolution of a hegemonic formation involves the reactivation of that contingency: the return from a "sublime" metaphoric fixation to a humble metonymic association.[29]

Laclau's point is that hegemony is the naturalization of a political order that has its origins in contingent—that is, localized and synchronic—practices. Political formations—trade unions, activist parties, racial groups—become stabilized when they serve to protect their interests and replicate a static matrix of self-identification, which Laclau identifies with metaphor. This self-replication is similar to what Jacques Rancière describes as the "policing" function of normative politics, when people ally with intact political names.[30] Lost in this metaphorical arrangement is the contingency that gave rise to political form in the first place, what Rancière describes as the aesthetic emergence of "dissensus," a contingency that was open to all sorts of forms and combinations of political alliance.[31]

For my purposes, there are several insights I wish to develop on the basis of Laclau's claim. Laclau's "hegemony" rings with Hames-García's "homogeny." Both signal the reification of a social identity beyond its origins, and its ultimate assignment as a static category within a political regime. Laclau and Hames-García are both interested in reactivating the dynamism of identity. It should be clear by now that this present book does not aim for "post-identity," any more than Laclau suggests we abandon metaphor and return to metonymy, or any more than Hames-García's account of identity is an abandonment of racial materialism. Indeed, for Hames-García and for this present book, recent critical renovations of materialism point the way for a return to place, to boundaries, to law and violence, to the material conditions that effect racialization. This is a return that is also an encounter with the very frameworks of racialization. We are by now well practiced at historicizing racialization, but such cultural histories often either leave race intact or attempt to leave it behind. Over the course of this book, I develop a sustained analytic for theorizing and discussing race and racialization, through the two axes of metaphor and metonymy. Returning to the pivot of a metonymically arranged identification into a metaphorically foreclosed racial assignment would be not only a look back in time but an encounter with the spatial arrangements and discursive assumptions that maintain a hegemonic status quo. Likewise, in the spirit of Laclau's critique, an examination of the material bases of group identification enables us to see how the often-imagined incongruity among identities can be traced back to certain points of origin, at which local differences were produced and then naturalized, so that "Jew," "black," and "Hispanic" can be thought of as distinct and incommensurate ways of being in a given city. I want to return, both in time and place, to the borders and lines of both division and connection.

The stakes of such a return would be the reactivation of a political scene of differentiation. As Laclau puts it, "using a Husserlian distinction, we could say that the social is equivalent to a *sedimented* order, while the political would involve the moment of *reactivation*."[32] Laclau's draw on Husserl is, for me, important for the present book's own borderline work, as I likewise attempt to move between an account of the enduring social reality of racialization and the more politically contingent, often fluid or active dissolution and recomposition of social identity. In Laclau's citation of Husserl, the social is static and the political is dynamic, and he aims to reactivate the former in order to mobilize the latter. In what follows, I grant that the social facts of identity formation matter; that is, they are made to matter by a range of strategies and techniques of control and domination. But I also consider the possibility that these materially arranged social identities may likewise be "reactivated," or rendered fluid and contingent, material but not inevitable. Doing so, we may retrieve a lost complexity in identity, as well as the force of identity's agency as an actor in social formation, and not simply society's object. I am thinking, for example, of Helena María Viramontes's *Their Dogs Came with Them*, a novel set during the high point of Chicano activism in Los Angeles, but also a novel in which none of the main characters self-consciously identifies as Chicano.[33] The characters hardly *reject* those social identities; they are just so deeply marginalized, so socially vulnerable, as to find no place in the matrix of social identification in the first place. At one point, a Chicana student activist gives Ben, a mentally ill, pariah-like character, her brown beret, and calls him *hermano*. Ben feels overwhelmed by the loving gesture, and wears the hat not because of the social identity it assigns him but because of the brotherhood it symbolizes. Elsewhere in the novel, Ben's sorrowful life seems to function as a stand-in for all sorts of ways of being dispossessed and cast aside in East L.A., so the extension of the brown beret to him expands the mutuality and recognition at work in the social identity "Chicano," locating the agency and dynamism of the local Chicano movement in a person whose trajectory of possibility is unpredictable.

The metaphorical and metonymical constitution of race has implications for the intersubjective relations that pertain to racial encounter, insofar as our sense of self is both self-contained and seemingly continuous, yet determined by others or contingent. How our identities are perceived and received by others matters. For instance, in both the phrase "black lives matter" and the reactionary rejoinder "all lives matter," we find a political theory and possibly an ethical corollary (unless it is the reverse). The former phrase demands political recognition of the materiality of race, and the latter seems to argue for liberal, individual accountability. Both amount to forms of recognition, with racial identity more or less advanced or occluded. I use *recognition* loosely here, simply to signal how all variations on identification amount to claims about the meaning of an identity in public life, and to suggest that identity and recognition are paired and in flux. White people who may not think of themselves as white on any given day may nonetheless recognize that they have a social benefit that comes with being white, a privilege that is wholly contingent on the production of race as a hierarchical system of value. That privilege is real, and it

cultural ambiguity, is captured in Gloria Anzaldúa's critical coinage of
"the borderlands" as a space of possibility. Anzaldúa famously argued
that "the Borderlands are physically present whenever two or more
cultures edge each other, where people of different races occupy the
same territory, where under, lower, middle and upper classes touch,
where the space between two individuals shrinks with intimacy."[36] Expanding on Anzaldúa's "borderlands," Mezzadra and Neilson coin the
term *borderscape* to account for the multiple functions and affordances
of the border, arguing that "isolating a single function of the border
does not allow us to grasp the flexibility of this institution. Nor does it
facilitate an understanding of the diffusion of practices and techniques
of border control within territorially bound spaces of citizenship and
their associated labor markets."[37] The border is an anxious frontier in
the war on terrorism; the border is the constitutive geography of law
and order; the border is the boundary between civilization and the
crime, drugs, poverty, and madness of everyplace else.

    In her meditation on form, Caroline Levine turns to the form-
less form of networks and juxtaposes the dynamism of the network
against what she understands to be the static formation of the border:
"Often operating outside of the logic of the nation-state, terrorists
have inspired nations to build ever-higher walls and other barriers to
try to exclude or contain them. Thus national boundaries continue to
operate powerfully—and sometimes more powerfully than ever—in
the face of transnational networks."[38] In Levine's account, the nation's
boundary is the opposite of a network, and that may be true from
the point of view of security experts. However, the point of network
theory is that networks territorialize boundaries, making them part
of their networks. Consider that the nationalist frenzy to build a wall
on the U.S.-Mexico border includes the desire to stop terrorists from
crossing over. In this regard, the border wall, which is and would be
far from impenetrable, becomes part of the larger map of terroristic
activity, a map of "terror-toriality," if I may. The wall may be built
on or proximate to the U.S.-Mexico border, but it exists as part of a

sprawling, tangled, discursive chain of political rhetoric, psychological paranoia, and economic anxiety that has come to dominate U.S.
and European nationalist politics in recent years, and that chain is
produced in part by a wider global phenomenon for which "terrorism" is but one link. Thought of that way, the wall would be both a
hard line against terrorist incursion and a zone of indeterminacy—the
space where terrorist ambition and terror-filled reaction join to remap
the nation. It is not only the case that "networks and enclosures are
constantly meeting," as Levine puts it, but that with both, the border
is simultaneously a boundary and a network, as well as a geography
of division and indeterminacy, and thus a space where the identity of
the nation is remapped and re-signified.[39] This is the terminal logic
of national sovereignty: borders are not simply the termination of the
nation, their boundaries, but the very logic of the nation, the nation's
center. In this way, "the border" betrays its promise of cartographical
precision, and perhaps comes to be geographically meaningless entirely,
functioning instead as an idea, and even more important, as discourse,
a rhetorical tool to leverage government spending on private prisons,
to increase police surveillance, and to generally trump up support for
a political agenda rooted in fear of enemy outsiders storming the gates.

I gesture to the U.S.-Mexico border by way of example, and to
ground this Introduction in geography, but this is a project more
about how we think about space and spacing than it is about national
sovereignty. The working hypothesis in this book will be that border
and line cooperate in spatial discourse analogous to how metaphor
and metonymy cooperate—not as distinct modes of separation, but
as figures of space, where each harbors the other. Similar to how a
racial name can function with some combination of metaphor and
metonymy, so too can spatial boundary markings suggest both homogenous, continuous spatial identity historically constituted across
time and the contiguous co-constitution of a given space with other
spaces, shifting its meaning according to a dynamic exchange of flux
and flow. To be a little taxonomic, then, the normative meaning of a

border is that it marks out a space of sovereignty, spatial identity, and
the outer limits of policing authority, while the transgressive meaning is that the border is the space where transient flows of culture and
commerce disrupt static sovereignty, where spatial identity becomes
hybridized, and where the policing function of politics (Rancière) is
challenged by the ethics of the sort of intimacy Anzaldúa suggests. The
line, by contrast, connects, provides access, and, quite different from
a border, occupies no space and is by definition unconstrained—lines
are infinite, and when Deleuze and Guattari coin the phrase "line of
flight," the line signals possibility rupturing forth from limitation.
Still, beyond these normative definitions and uses of line, *line* also
metaphorically signals containment, constraint, and division. W. E. B.
Dubois famously named "the color line" as the preeminent problem
of the twentieth century, speaking to an enduring division separating
and even constitutive of black and white. I juxtapose *border* and *line*
with the hypothesis that in situations when the normative definition
of one term is in play, the transgressive definition of the other is likewise in play, and the rest of this book is a study in the conditions by
which the one gives way to the other.

Though the book is organized into chapters, with each chapter
focused on a discrete place, a specific group, and strategies for place-
making, its overall conception is more like that of an essay, with a
running through-line not so much of argument as of inquiry. If categorical identities are composed of several different, sometimes incommensurate arrangements of space—if space can be said to be more than
one thing at once and to be experienced in simultaneously different
ways—then an essay on identity and space cannot move toward certain conclusions while discarding others, nor can it ground itself in
a single theoretical method at the expense of others. Instead, such an
essay must proceed by discovering the proliferating modes of space-
making and the refracting processes of identity formation at work in
a particular set of circumstances. This sort of discovery of protean but
traceable processes is signaled in the title *The Border and the Line*, in

which the two nouns are near synonyms even as they signal different operations with respect to space. The correlative object and motif in this book is the freeway which, it turns out, is likewise two things at once, never entirely self-same: a boundary line for the L.A. Eruv, a border line for Watts and East L.A., a conduit for Budd Schulberg's workshop, and a space of improvisatory resignification for the narrator of Paul Beatty's *The Sellout*. If there's an argument here, it is for that sort of multiplicity, though let me immediately and clearly check the tendency to leap from multiplicity to the meaningless proliferation of possibility and thus the decentering of experiences of racialization. Here, the multiple agencies of something like a freeway account for the holistic if highly fractured means by which whiteness and blackness (say) come into being through interrelated if incommensurate processes of racialization.

This book frequently doubles back on itself and revisits its own terms because its subjects—race, space, and Los Angeles—do the same. To cite but one example, Jewishness becomes immaterial and universal for Budd Schulberg in the second chapter, and rematerializes as a highly sectarian quasi-privatized control of public space in the third chapter. That change is not linear. The secular universalism of Schulberg's Jewishness, and the presumption of total access to Los Angeles across the network of freeways—and indeed, the desire for everyone to have equal access *beyond race*—remains a dream for some, even as groups working in the name of Jewishness address structural racism and racial inequity. These three kinds of Jewishness—the universal, the sectarian, and the revolutionary—operate more or less within the same space, though each imagines the space of encounter with the other in radically distinct ways. Accounting for these synchronic differences requires this book to make multiple passes across its objects. Another way of putting all of this is that the book is recursive, though not redundant, as it circles back around to key locales, textual passages, and critical motifs.

Critical motifs refers to a critical principle or idea that recurs across different works associated with a given school of thought. The freeway as a tool of racial sequestration appears commonly across materialist theorizations of cities, for instance.[40] The space of encounter, variously imagined as ethical or political, is a common motif in theories of the neighbor. In *The Border and the Line* I do not privilege one particular theory of space over another but put several in conversation with each other across the chapters. The chief theoretical query is how to think about the materiality of space alongside theories of the intersubjective encounters that happen within space. *Materiality* here signals the built environment, including the racial and economic motivations for building it, while *encounters* are those political and ethical engagements that occur within and across spaces, and that are very often determined by those spaces. Of course, this could be phrased in the opposite way: spaces are built precisely to arrange some kinds of encounter while obliterating others, as any gated neighborhood makes clear. It's not simply a question of linking a material theory of space with a political theory of encounter, but of understanding how each may be shot through with the other.

Henri Lefebvre's challenge to philosophers to engage with the material dimensions and indeed the materialization of space provides an unexpected critical motif, which I cite across this book. Lefebvre imagines the philosopher of space as a tightrope walker, giving the thrill of risking a mentally tricky task while remaining poised up above and beyond his object of study. Calling philosophy the tightrope walk which risks nothing, he suggests that the truly daring task is to take on the complicated dynamism of the material elements of space as they are determined by political economy. True enough, though it must be said that there are very few actual *people* in Lefebvre's tome, and the same can be said for theories of the neighbor cited across this book: the neighbor as ethical subject is omnipresent in these theories, but actual neighborhoods in actual space are rare indeed. So I do not lean over-heavily on any given theorist or even any given, broadly framed school of thought, but, to ironize Lefebvre, walk the tightrope back and forth, a thin line between the object of space and the subject of neighbor.

I have arranged the chapters to produce a tension between ethical and political claims about neighbor relations, and to substantiate the efficacy of discursive and materialist engagements with racial inequality, on the way to an argument for their cooperation in comparative critical race studies. Chapter 1 ends with the book's most hopeful conclusion, and by putting it first rather than last, I play the book counter to type. It is common for books about race and ethnicity to look for the upbeat note at the end, but I regard this as a critical trap that would clamp down on the more multidimensional if more difficult-to-reckon-with insights of any account of race. Evading the trap, I begin with the optimistic affordance of metaphor and its correlative ethics in the first chapter, only to turn to the more materialist politics of metonymy in the second chapter. The first chapter examines how metaphorical and other imaginative community-building practices may override the political dead ends of material space, but this can be only a starting point for material redress, and in the second chapter I argue that Schulberg is overinvested in the redemptive capacity of metaphor, and only effects change when he becomes proximate to the material reality of the impoverished ghetto. Chapter 3 navigates metaphor and metonymy together and explicitly argues for the clear-eyed combination of them in analyses of racial formation, especially in accounts of race and place.

Each chapter is structured with a long investigation of a particular story or episode in a specific neighborhood, followed by a closing section that tests the opening section's investigations. Chapter 1, "Redlining and Realigning in East L.A.: The Neighborhoods of Helena María Viramontes and *Union de Vecinos*," takes on a fundamental question for literature scholars: What are the borders of identity between reader and text? By way of an answer, I argue that we become the neighbor to the literature, and I follow with an exploration of the philosophical and material implications of that neighboring. The chapter's focus is East Los Angeles, a predominantly low-income, Latino quarter of the city. In the 1930s through the 1950s, the East L.A. neighborhood of Boyle

Heights was a multiethnic, low-income, politically active community, demographically frozen due to redlining housing policies that made it difficult for residents to relocate. A good deal of historiography has been published on Boyle Heights's politically interesting past, and current journalism tends to romanticize the area, but the real neighborhood is a dynamically negotiated space, with shifting lines of belonging and exclusion. I examine Helena María Viramontes's novel *Their Dogs Came with Them*, set in Boyle Heights at the peak of its gang wars in the 1970s, and I also explore the real neighborhood, including the activist project *Union de Vecinos*, a socialist organizing collective inspired by liberation theology to reclaim the neighborhood, from both the gangs and reactionary policing, in the name of social justice. This chapter develops the material implications of existing theories of the "neighbor" in order to argue for a radical conception of neighborhood ethics. Ethics in Viramontes's novel exist as metaphorical gestures, when the strangeness of another enables productive forms of encounter. Likewise, my analysis of the *Union de Vecinos*'s neighborhood organizing examines the metaphorical efficacy of liberation theology for resignifying a politics of law into a politics of love. Neighborhood boundaries such as police curfews and gang-tags compose Boyle Heights in *Their Dogs*, and *Union de Vecinos* likewise "marks" its neighborhood with spray-painted safe-zone inscriptions, and through spatial negotiations with gangs. This chapter analyzes the function and effect of these boundary markers, and advances a theory of the neighborhood.

Chapter 2, "The Matter of the Neighbor and the Property of 'Unmitigated Blackness,'" considers property as the material and psychical grounds of American racism. The majority of this chapter explores the Watts Writers Workshop, founded in the heart of Watts by Budd Schulberg immediately after the Watts Rebellion of 1965, and argues that the success and final demise of the project is traceable to Schulberg's real estate transactions on behalf of the Workshop.[41] Schulberg was an Oscar-winning screenwriter and author of several popular novels, and his status as a white, Jewish resident of Beverly Hills was a source of constant suspicion for critics of the Workshop. But Schulberg maintained that he was learning to "think black" through his financial and sweat-equity investments in Watts, going so far as to lease and renovate property to house Workshop writers. Schulberg eventually founded Frederick Douglass House, a charitable foundation and a physical building for black creative arts. Drawing on Schulberg's archives, including lease contracts, letters, and personal notes, I argue that Schulberg's personal and financial investment in Watts relocated his political standing as the "neighbor" to the Watts writers with whom he worked. The catch is that being a neighbor subjected Schulberg to political marginality and police harassment, culminating in the FBI sabotage of the Workshop (it was burned down by an admitted FBI plant in 1975). Schulberg never fully understood his outsider-insider status, a claim I substantiate through a careful reading of a conversation between Schulberg and James Baldwin in which Baldwin is able to peel back the multiple layers of identity sustaining whiteness's controlling claims on black property. Both writers hit upon "love" as the only way to cut through the Gordian knot of racism binding the nation, and I turn to passages from Baldwin's *The Fire Next Time* and *No Name in the Street* for his thesis about love, race, and democracy.[42] I close this chapter with a study of Paul Beatty's recent, painfully funny Los Angeles novel, *The Sellout* (2015), in which love is ironized and black Angelenos assert an atavistic claim on property, with segregation, plantations, and the return of slavery. The novel is set in "Dickens," based on the real community of Richland, a one-hundred-twenty-year-old farm tract persisting in the heart of Compton. Beatty's novel explores the cartography of Los Angeles's racial identities, alighting on lines of the map as the most distinguishing and potentially valuable forms of racial identification.

Chapter 3, "My Neighborhood: Private Claims, Public Space, and Jewish Los Angeles," argues for the emergence of privately held ethics in the formation of neighborhood publics. The chapter primarily focuses on Jewish neighborhoods, including the L.A. Eruv, the largest in the West. An *eruv* is an area with boundaries designated by a rabbinical authority to constitute domestic rather than public space for all Jews living within. *Eruv* is Hebrew for "mixture," and it involves mixing public and private spaces into one large "courtyard" or domestic enclosure. This is typically done by stringing a thin wire across existing lighting, telephone, and traffic posts, and by designating freeway barrier walls as doorways. The wire is all but invisible from street level, but when it circumscribes a space—over eighty square miles in the case of the L.A. Eruv—the Jews living within it are permitted to treat it as domestic space according to the Sabbath laws, facilitating a range of practical conveniences. This chapter will explore the political implications of this mixture of public and private and sacred and secular spaces, especially in relation to Chapter 1's study of political theology in East L.A. In addition, I argue that the eruv is a "counter-public" for the Orthodox Jews it circumscribes, but that the public alignment of "Jewish" with "Orthodox" eclipses other kinds of Jewish publics in Los Angeles. The chapter forays beyond L.A. to examine a plurality of Jewish concepts of the neighborhood in a recent short documentary, *My Neighbourhood*, about secular Israeli Jews who partner with Muslim Palestinians to protest Orthodox Jewish appropriation of Palestinians' homes.[43] I draw insights from that film back into a study of the L.A. Eruv, and compare the Jewish strategies for making a neighborhood with the strategies at work in Boyle Heights. Both the eruv and the *Union de Vecinos* countertagging project are counter-cartographies, in which alternative maps of possibility and community are traced across the city, and both suggest new conceptions of community within neighborhoods.

In the Conclusion, "Love, Space, and the Grounds of Comparative Ethnic Literature Study," I discuss my own interpolation by the map of Jewish Los Angeles, as I write about my family's Los Angeles itinerary. My mother's mother was Salvadoran, and her father a Sephardic Jew, and I write about the family's postwar movement, from Boyle Heights to MacArthur Park, to Pico-Robertson—neighborhoods of ethnic distinction, wherein this mixed family blended in with various communities.

My parents eventually settled in a very white section of Orange County, and the Conclusion begins with a reflection on the relative durability of identity, and especially the role of geography for sustaining or constraining a positive identification with race and ethnicity. Following this personal examination of race and space, I argue for the value of a close, comparative analysis in ethnic studies and ethnic literature study. Turning to the metaphor of the neighborhood once more, I argue that precisely because different racial and ethnic groups occupy the same space at the same time, or come into contact through economic and imaginative borderzones, we miss the vital co-constitution of racial identities when we do not compare. Moreover, if we are to remain committed to a discourse of identity in literature study, the book in general and the Conclusion in particular argue that we must account for identity's origins in material space. Comparative study itself is the neighborhood we make as teachers and scholars, but this conceptual neighborhood must engage real-life neighborhoods in the world around. Without wishing to polemicize against trends toward globalizing American studies or the trend toward "deep history," I nonetheless make a second argument that synchronic analysis of a given space and time is vital for understanding how literature and other forms of cultural production are part of a network with the world around. Though the book draws widely across different theoretical statements, here I rely firmly on Bruno Latour's sustained explanation of "networks" for charting how identities are formed in space and time, and for placing literature into conversation with that formation. My third argument is about how reading, researching, and teaching are the means by which literature enters the world. Returning to "love," I argue that love and its attendant commitments of recognition and responsibility have a place in our writing and our teaching.

CHAPTER 1

REDLINING AND REALIGNING IN EAST L.A.

The Neighborhoods of Helena María Viramontes and Union de Vecinos

"If miracle really is the favorite child of belief, then its father has been neglecting his paternal duties badly, at least for some time."

Franz Rosenzweig, *The Star of Redemption*[1]

HOW CAN WE COMPARE—literatures, cultures, places, people—without collapsing difference into sameness? How do we maintain specificity and the contingency of experience, even while seeking some understanding across experiences? This is a comparative book to the core, but one that resists stabilizing its terms of comparison from chapter to chapter, across race and space. Indeed, a running argument across the chapters is that the efficacy of comparison is in its query of stable categories. Granted, especially in academia but also in civic life, social identities, cultures, and the modicum of political power that goes with them are hard fought and won, and it would be a glib project that sought to deconstruct them. Rather then, a comparative query should return to the very grounds of what was fought for in the first place. On the other hand, we must not assume that we will find some facile common bases for comparison, some key term, critical phrase, or even physical location that will establish a baseline commonality. It is not that I think black, Chicano, and Jewish

literatures and neighborhoods are so different as to have nothing in
common, but neither do I presume that each has equivalent access
to or juxtaposition within anything that would be common among
all three, be it some philosophical idea (love, justice, human being)
or material experience (chiefly the assigning of value through the
distribution of space). As has been amply demonstrated elsewhere,
African Americans, Jews, and Mexican Americans have encountered
and contributed to the American racial imaginary from different
historical trajectories, and with different kinds of investments in
nationalist identification. This is particularly true for these minority
communities in the western states, with Jews migrating west in the
late nineteenth century as part of a teleological project of American identification: European Jewish merchants and scholars would
become Americans through pastoral engagement with the frontier.[2]
This migration is coeval with and contrapuntal to the experiences of
Mexicans in the United States, who were having their land usurped
from them through violence and legal shenanigans at the very same
time. Black migration to Southern California accelerated during
World War II, and needless to say, recent arrivals encountered a city
that was very much formed through a prior half-century of racial
struggles, though this whole story could be told in reverse, as there is
no concept of "the American West" that is not already tangled with
broader American ideas and practices of racialization.[3]

These different histories and spatial trajectories lead to unequal and
perhaps incommensurable relations to Los Angeles; even as Jews, Chicanos, and African Americans live in the same city at the same time,
crossing the same boundaries of the same neighborhoods, they may
have dramatically different experiences of racialization. A synchronic
comparative study such as the following, therefore, needs to query
not only the experiences of the different groups involved but also the
several key terms that would seem to be common to each, but which
are encountered and engaged in critically different ways. These key
terms are indeed the very ones that would seem to suggest the logic of

the comparison in the first place: the city, its neighborhoods, and the boundaries among them. Not only are specific ethnic neighborhoods different from one another, the very terms *race, recognition, neighborhood,* and the several terms designating the borders and lines of communities—from maps to police districts to freeway walls—ought to be investigated at the very moment they are invoked. To that end, a comparative study should attempt to understand the groups in question as well as the putative basis of the comparison itself.

Thomas Claviez makes a similar methodological point in a forum essay in *PMLA* on comparative literature study.[4] Claviez correctly observes that the often unacknowledged master trope of comparative literature is metaphor, when an assumed third term universalizes and unifies two otherwise different bodies of literature. In comparative literature study, that third term might be *narrative,* or *form,* or *modernism;* in comparative ethnic studies, the third term might be *neighborhood,* and with both ventures, the metaphorical third term is the basis for the comparison itself, whether it is of French and Arabic novels, or of Chicano and Jewish neighborhoods. Claviez argues for a reassessment of the ethics of comparative study organized by the figure of metonymy: proximity, contiguity, and difference instead of distance, simultaneity, and substitutability. Elsewhere I have written in particular agreement with Claviez, alighting on "proximity" as a basis of an ethics of recognition, and in general this book bears out Claviez and others' valorization of metonymy, certainly in Chapter 2, on writing projects associated with Watts and South Central Los Angeles.[5] However, this first chapter examines metaphor not as the assumed third term bridging over difference, but as something more akin to miracle, when metaphors are not the easy givens of comparison but the difficult work of imagination, a way of seeing what *might be* through the lens of *what is.*

Turning to metaphor, imagination, and a raft of resources not typically used for analyzing Chicana/o literature, including, it must be said, several Jewish theorists and philosophers, should not suggest a swerve away from the political salience of Chicano identity, or the politics emerging from immediate and localized contexts. As will be clear further on, for my purposes in this chapter metaphor is bound up with metonymy, and political names or movements that function as signifying common "third terms" uniting groups of individuals are traceable back to their metonymical origins. This is Ernesto Laclau's basic claim for the political efficacy and agency of these forms. Laclau contends that the force of political agency that comes from naming a group originates in its material conditions, its grounding in space and time. This is why we do well to recall the Chicano Movement's origins in East L.A., and to specify the material conditions early movement organizers were protesting, namely brutal policing, poorly funded social and public services, education policy that aimed at cultural erasure, and racist real estate practices. The name *Chicano* bears with it its political origins, or it ought to. For Laclau, when political names become "social," or otherwise habiliments easily put on or taken off, they become simply metaphors— perhaps what Rorty calls "dead metaphors"—losing their political capacity.[6] Indeed, they become terms of identity whose boundaries are incessantly policed on the basis of easy symbolism or empty gestures. Laclau would have us return to the material contingencies that give rise to political names in the first place, which may mean emphasizing less identity and more identification, or the contingent process by which people begin to make claims on experiences and come to know themselves as part of something larger in space and time. It must be said, identification is the doorway to metaphor, as it allows for substitutions. To see yourself in a social name or in the life experiences of another suggests that there are elements of your experience that are transposable from person to person. And perhaps, as I argue in this chapter, the next step is committing to materialize the space of justice and equality that would sustain that sort of mutuality.

METAPHORS HAPPEN

If a metaphor appears in a novel and no one notices it, does it still carry meaning? Near the end of Helena María Viramontes's novel, *Their Dogs Came with Them*,[7] a sign of the Virgin Mary, Our Lady of Guadalupe, appears as a faint narrative etching. The teenager Turtle, a girl who passes as a boy to secure status in a violent gang, is being hunted by enemies from all quarters and contemplating taking hold of a thin lifeline, a job offered to her if she can show up for work at sunrise. Hiding out in an East Los Angeles cemetery, Turtle digs through a trashcan for something edible and finds instead an old bouquet of flowers, signs of death that she stuffs into her leather jacket for padding and warmth. Later, when she finds an open crypt for shelter, she unzips her jacket and lets the flowers fall to the ground:

The parchments of flowers tumble to the floor and all around her ankles. Bunches and bushes of old carnations and roses and gardenias and magnolias and baby's breath, reduced to their brittle bone stems, still carried a trace of transient perfumes. All the bunches together, the petals and leaves and stems, created enough padding for a bed. (236)

Her "bed" is in a tomb, and the space and the "brittle bone stems" foreshadow her death a few chapters later, yet the tumble of flowers from her coat may call to mind other flowers, the miraculous roses that symbolize the Virgin Mary of Guadalupe. In 1531, Mary appeared at Tepeyac to Juan Diego, the indigenous Mexican convert to Catholicism, and told him to ask the bishop to build a church in her name. The bishop asked for a miraculous sign, and Mary directed Juan Diego to gather roses, which were blooming out of season, in his cloak and to present them to the bishop. When Juan Diego tumbled the roses before the bishop, the image of Mary was imprinted on the inside of the cloak, a sign confirming the symbol of the roses, which in turn signify Mary as "Our Lady of Guadalupe." When Turtle opens her jacket, spilling the flowers, her gesture recalls that miracle.

Or does it? The question of verifiability shifts—not, "Did the *miracle* happen"? but "Did the *metaphor* happen"? And how *do* metaphors "happen"? In Viramontes's novel, there is no narrative tip-off, no clear annunciation of similarity between Turtle and Mary, and the flowers quickly become an abject "bed" for Turtle.[8] Pressed up against the marble engraving, "Asleep in Jesus, Blessed Sleep," Turtle is both a subject of grace and marked for death. Turtle never does show up for her job in the morning and is drawn into a drug-fueled gang murder instead, and her concluding violence is less a willed malevolence than an acquiescence, not the primacy of the animal ("Turtle") self over the divinely human but rather an exhausted submission to the ecology of death of which she has already become a part, the Marian metaphor a weightless shimmer with no obviously grounded referent. With no direction from the narrator, it is up to the reader to read the Marian typology and sustain Turtle as someone who, despite her violence, growing social abjection, and concluding nihilism, is—miraculously—a subject of some sort of grace. The affecting resonance between *la guadalupana* and Turtle in the cemetery suggests how both miracle and metaphor are the effects of a receptive reader whose own readiness to read forms a network with the novel, obviating supernatural intercession.[9]

Miracle is typically considered to be an interruption of everyday reality, a rupture of ontology, presumably by some force of the divine. In this chapter I swap the divine for a concept of radical alterity, in which ruptures are not *caused* by that alterity but *are* that alterity, and similarly, in which metaphors are figural gestures toward some other way of being, encoded in but finally imagined beyond given material reality. Beginning this way, I consider metaphor not simply as the familiar term lending its meaning to the unfamiliar but as the promise that something can be other than what it seems. This may be thought of as the transformation of being into becoming, as in the work of Bergson, Deleuze, and Grosz (among others), or as the collapse of the dualisms of experience and knowledge or even matter and spirit found in theories of new materialism, in which imagination, belief, and spirit are indistinct from cognitive reality.[10] In this way, contrary to accounts of Magical Realism, in which the supernatural is assimilated into reality within the literary text, the rupture of the miracle remains unabsorbed and a problem for characters and the reader alike.[11] If a new account of reality is to emerge from miracle's rupture, it will have to figure what I am calling "reality's otherwise," which the miracle occasions and which the metaphor represents. Coming to terms with reality's otherwise is necessarily an ethical act, for it means taking responsibility for the consequences of reading's rupture, rather than simply assigning it to fiction. As Gayatri Spivak puts it, "[T]he figure of the experience of the impossible *is* the condition of [the] possibility of deciding. In the aporia or double bind, to decide is the burden of responsibility."[12] "Responsibility," in this case, means sustaining love for the seemingly unlovable. One character suggests what this chapter will argue. Writing about a homeless woman, who appears across *Their Dogs*, the college student Ben thinks, "*one would need metaphor to love her*" (125).[13] Reading is a form of decision making, as Spivak puts it, and love is a choice to believe in the possibility of the world figured forth by the text, including the choice to insist on that possibility as part and parcel of the real world.[14]

Metaphor's relation to the material, immanent world is a prominent subtext in rhetorical theory. Romantic conceptions of metaphor would have language transport a reader beyond the real, into a state of imagination, reaching an apotheosis, Kant maintained, in the sublime. In the same grain, Nietzsche theorized that *all* language was metaphorical, that we err insofar as we conflate our language of things with things themselves (and so more or less, goes the deconstructive account of writing, through Derrida and de Man).[15] In functionalist terms, Kenneth Burke explains that metaphor's comparative work allows us to see the "'thisness' of a 'that,'" or to locate common properties among the metaphor and its referent.[16] Especially helpful is Richard Rorty's concept of metaphors as tools of communication that, when we repeat them often enough, become part of everyday speech (think of rain clouds and silver linings). Rorty's account of metaphor downplays literature's generative capacity, but he does allow for metaphor to be something like a rupture—a break from everyday speech and an introduction of something truly new that we then struggle to assimilate into the reality it ruptured.[17] In Viramontes's novel, metaphors are indeed ruptures, or departures from the material real wherein they occur, but they are not flights away from the real and in fact can only make sense with further reference to the real. Juan Diego's *tilma* is physically imprinted with the image of Mary, and that image is Viramontes's metaphor. In this way, *Their Dogs* evades the presumed opposition between romantic and realist literature (or poetry and prose) described by Roman Jakobson, not by transcending the material real but by tethering the imaginative possibility of another futurity to the lived experience of characters and even readers.[18] Metaphors are not objects that simply appear in literature but are phenomena contingent on a reader's anticipation and affirmation. This dialectical relation, between the metaphors consciously and unconsciously patterned in texts and the receptivity of readers to notice those metaphors, sustains the possibility of imagining and potentially creating other conceptions of history and community: this is reality's otherwise. The miracle occurs to the extent that a reader bears a vision of another, better way of being in the world and seeks to make it real.

LIKE A CRACK IN THE SIDEWALK

Their Dogs Came with Them takes place in an East Los Angeles neighborhood that is isolated from the rest of the city by a network of freeways, bridges, and cemetery walls. Housing is dense, and the noise, pollution, and violence of urban and industrial life constitute a toxic ecology for the poor, abandoned, and often feared characters of the novel. The novel is set in 1960, the year L.A. County began bulldozing parts of the neighborhood to lay concrete for freeways, and 1970, when the L.A. county sheriff imposed curfews to stall the Chicano Moratorium.[19] The curfews targeted suspected Chicano student activists, and the novel's characters are constantly under siege by violent policing and governmental dehumanization. The attack on public citizenship is underscored in the novel by a fictional rabies outbreak among stray dogs: "From First Street to Boyle to Whittier and back to Pacific Boulevard . . . roadblocks enforced a quarantine to contain a potential outbreak of rabies" (54). Anyone living in the quarantine zone has to remain indoors after dark, while the Quarantine Authority (QA) goes on air and foot patrol, shooting "undomesticated mammals" (54). The novel's title refers to an epigraph from Miguel Leon-Portilla's *The Broken Spears*, which describes the sixteenth-century arrival of Spanish colonial soldiers, wearing mail, carrying muskets, and attended by dogs.[20] In the novel's present time, the dogs have slipped their historical leash, no longer instruments of colonialism, roaming, rather, as signs of domination under regimes of biopower and government control, and all the characters maintain some metonymic relation to the dog, a sign of both vulnerability and containment.

Switching back and forth between the specific years 1960 and 1970, there is no narrated "between time" in the novel. As a result, we see the major characters as children and then as teens or young adults, whose lives are ever more deeply embedded in the grain of the neighborhood. Tranquilina, who meets Turtle twice in the novel, is an evangelical Christian missionary whose outer face of piety and care masks dread and doubt: a survivor of a brutal rape, she cannot forget the taste of dirt in her mouth as she was shoved on the ground, nor the smell of the "manure man" who assaulted her, and her missionary commitment to the abject of East L.A. is confounded by the abject experience of her trauma. To make matters even more challenging for Tranquilina, she is vexed by a promise her mother made when she was pregnant with her. Tranquilina's parents fled from peonage in Mexico and were lost in the desert during their migration north, with Tranquilina's mother fatigued and in labor. Her mother prayed for salvation, and her father

drew on ancestral forces to fly beyond the canyon walls to scout for
water and safe passage. Tranquilina struggles with this story—could it
be a metaphor for strength and faith in the family? Or do her parents
expect her to believe in the miracle that her father really is a *voladore*,
descendant of Aztecs, composed of lizard skin and hollow bird bones?
In either case, Tranquilina's missionary work, dedicated to helping the
outcasts of Los Angeles, seems to fulfill her mother's promise. Here
the distinction between human and animal is displaced by the more
salient distinction between exhaustion and endurance, and miracle and
metaphor converge as equally improbable supplements to the reality
Tranquilina witnesses all around.

The character whose circuit most frequently intersects with the
others is a nameless homeless woman, who bears a mental map of back
alleys brimming with rotten food, homeless shelters, soup kitchens,
and the routines of stray dogs who will inevitably lead her to a free if
spoiled meal. She is described as a composition of the streets, with her
layers of castaway clothes covering her own flake-away skin, but when
she faints in a missionary soup kitchen, Tranquilina's mother is sure
it's the miraculous spirit of God taking hold of her body.

As characters constantly navigate the city's borders and boundaries, they must also negotiate the people associated with those places.
Viramontes creates a narrative effect whereby characters encounter
each other as both subjects and objects of the neighborhood, real
people with limitless and terrifying depth as well as residual artifacts
of a neighborhood in ruins. The narrative plants a number of physical
elements that become metonymically linked with particular characters in those precise places but which other characters transform into
metaphors of meaning. For instance, Turtle comes across a graffiti tag
left by her brother, missing in Vietnam. Turtle is haunted by her in-
authentic and now severed "brotherhood," despite transforming herself
from Antonia Maria, with long hair and dresses, into "ass-kicking"
Turtle, with shaved head and a leather jacket. The tag marks a physical
as well as psychical border zone, and though it materially demarcates

sanctuary, the emotions she metonymically associates with it crack open Turtle's "shell." While Turtle idles, lost in her own thought, the homeless woman accidentally careens into Turtle's personal space. "He must have been there all along like a crack in the sidewalk," the woman thinks, a simile that reduces Turtle to the street itself, though she quickly revises herself as she "recognized his smell of the streets and looked into the slits of his eyes and she raised a trembling finger to her parched lips to hush any thoughts of him hurting her" (83). The "smell of the streets" seems to confirm the association with the "crack in the sidewalk," but where the former reduces Turtle to an object of the neighborhood, the latter suggests their shared status as homeless people, and the woman's gesture for quiet makes her the oddly maternal figure to Turtle's terrified child.

Turtle, in fact, is terrified. She had been reflecting on the frayed bonds of loyalty between her and her brother, and in his absence she is beset by all her earliest fears, of enemy gangs, the violence within her own gang, her abandonment by her family, and the ghosts of the long dead, whose interred bodies were said to be dug up and plowed under to make way for the freeways.[21] When she is interrupted by the homeless woman, Turtle takes her to be the angel of death herself:

And just as Luis Lil Lizard had warned, the death mask tripped and her bag of bones tocked and Turtle froze, scared shitless, shitless, can you believe it? Just death and Turtle inside the round bright jar of lamppost light, nothing else surrounding them but night. (218)

Turtle does not melt away into the mist, as the homeless woman perceives, but flees, her internal voice screaming in fear of this ghostly apparition of all she has dreaded.

Encounters such as these are *not* instances of recognition. The homeless woman has no idea why her gesture works and remains haunted by the meeting for the rest of the night. As much as the anticipated attack, the letting be yields an uncanny dispossession for each. This may be because characters (there are more, noted further on) know themselves to be psychically fractured, afraid, hungry, composed of and imposed upon by the city but presume the other is simply a unified agent of malevolence. The letting be and even subsequent acts of generosity among characters unsettle the fictive reality that was a basis for enduring in the world and make it hard for a reader easily to classify any given character. The homeless woman, who had been searching trash cans for food before she encountered Turtle, feels a deep loneliness, punctured by her hunger, and she returns to shadowing a dog hoping it will lead her to food. She briefly walks *with* the dog, just as she was briefly *with* Turtle, and each instance suggests a commonality, even as that commonality resists transforming into sameness or equivalence. To put it another way, the metonymy of the dog does not materialize into a metaphor, nor are Turtle and the homeless woman the same, though for each, exposure, vulnerability, and the body's needs are common experiences.[22]

Metonymy's efficacy is its capacity to locate people in place, accounting for the pressure of material objects and environmental and ecological constraints. Cracks in the sidewalk, freeway underpasses, mobile quarantine zones, roaming dogs, and spray paint tags turn out to be consequential, possibly the difference between life and death. The environment has a kind of agency, directing flows of people on paths of danger or safety before they are even aware of it, or making people suddenly aware of a social complexity previously unnoticed.[23] These are the "fatal contiguities" Hsuan Hsu describes in his account of *Their Dogs*, though the lateral dimension of *contiguity* only tells half the story.[24] Metonymy's materialist function is the grounds for more imaginative association, hinged to but not grounded by material objects. Turtle appears "like a crack in the sidewalk" for the homeless woman, and if the simile-as-metonymy deepens the association of Turtle with the street, it also demonstrates how spaces transmogrify and new, possibly terrifying worlds erupt from the cracks. Material place bears a psychical depth, and psychically complex subjects are also objects of material consequence. In the space of the neighborhood, people are locatable, legible, but also liable to misreading. The home-less woman's proximity to Turtle means she has to read him—that is, locate him as part of her neighborhood, of which she, too, is a part. Likewise, Turtle sees the homeless woman "trip," as if over a crack in the sidewalk, and so the two are psychically, not to mention meta-phorically, linked by this material rupture.

The character Ben, who forecasts the efficacy of metaphor as a ve-hicle for "love," exemplifies this cooperation of metonymy and meta-phor. As Hsu observes, Ben falls asleep during a night of writing and wakes with his own words smudged on his cheek. In effect, he becomes metonymically stamped by his own text.[25] Later, when Tranquilina is searching for Ben, she sees approximations of him in the homeless and marginal men living under freeways and sleeping in back alleys, draw-ing on his example as a far more salient vehicle for understanding the lives of her neighbors than the general bromides of religion.[26] If Ben fails to find the loving metaphor, he nonetheless becomes a figuration of metaphor itself. That fusion of text and face envisions the impos-sible, the collapsing of the gap between presence and writing, or the attempt to make writing the vehicle for loving the life of another. The struggle to see the face of the other, the primal scene of recognition, necessarily fails, and that failure is written across Ben's own face as a palimpsest that writes over but neither conceals nor reveals the life already inscribed there.

At the same time, the supplemental inscription has a genealogy in the novel, if we credit the Marian metaphor of Turtle's jacket full of flowers, and though Mary is only obliquely referenced in the novel, her example is instructive here. According to Juan Diego's witness, Mary appeared as a young, Aztec-seeming woman, speaking *Nahuatl*, underscoring at once her singularity and her ubiquity and interchange-ability. The roses she helped Juan Diego gather were necessary signs for the incredulous bishop, who would not credit Juan Diego's own testament. And the enduring miracle, visible still, is the imprint of Mary's image on Juan Diego's cloak, revealed upon delivering the flowers. The miraculous imprint is metonymic, yet it is a metonym of Mary, whose appearance itself is metaphorical—a figuration of motherhood, beneficence, and conquest. The metaphor's necessary legibility suggests how reality bears within it the possibility of being otherwise.

At stake in this review is the status of metaphor as described earlier but also the very question of the miracle. If there is no metaphor, there is no outside to the text, nothing beyond what the characters see and feel and experience. Likewise, there would be no possibility for a miracle, which in this case does not simply mean no godly revelation but no possibility for a rupture of the world as it appears. Is Ben nothing but a metonymy, a character whose significance is in his situatedness, making him indistinct from all the other similarly situated and marginal figures across the novel? Is Turtle, like a crack in the sidewalk, finally reducible to the streets? Or is there a gesture toward something beyond—call it imagination, hope, possibility, transformation, all of which are troped by the miracle—both within the text and outside of it, a gesture for the reader to recover?

Turtle's itinerary after fleeing the homeless woman is an instructive exploration of the production of that outside space through imagination. From her spot under the street light, she flees to the cemetery, but before she sleeps among the dead and the blessed, her hunger drives her across the street to the Val-U-Mart, where she has a complex encounter with the store owner, Ray. Ray smells Turtle's unwashed body, sees the hunger written on her face, and fearfully fumbles for his pistol beneath the counter. His panic peaks when she hands him a quarter and asks for a candy bar, as he thinks it can only be a ruse to get him to open the cash register, but she simply pays for the candy bar and tears into it.

Up to this point, Ray senses the potential violence that the end of the novel will confirm: hunger, exhaustion, and fading endurance suggest to him the limited possibilities for this gang member. He is not wrong; Turtle will kill and be killed in a few hours. But he also reads the legible scrim of another kind of life. Recalling his own experience of humiliation and deprivation as a child of Japanese descent deported to an internment camp, Ray "realized he had not witnessed such hunger, though he had lived too long a life to deny its existence," and on the spot, he offers her a job, provided she can show up the following morning at 7 a.m. The narrative explanation of Ray's surprising offer pivots from metonymic to metaphorical possibilities: "Maybe it was the achy spasms of his back as he approached the double doors. Maybe it was his bad heart, or maybe his good heart. Maybe he wanted to be kind, or maybe employ one of their kind" (260). The narration further tropes on Ray's own exhausted body as a figure for empathy:

Maybe he thought about dust and how he ate it at every meal, slept with it between the sheets, had breathed in the dust storms like smoke. Maybe because Ray understood way too well how everything could be taken away in one signature, one Executive Order 9066, and all that was left were the clothes on his back, and nothing, nothing else except perhaps for someone's kindness, a memory which still made him weep. (260–261)

His life thus becomes a viable comparison: a known experience gives access to an unknown life and enables him to do what was unimaginable to him moments before. Ray does not so much identify with Turtle as simply take stock of what her body betrays beyond her identity: cold, wet, hunger, the too-small clothes, and the smell of the streets are comprehensible to Ray not as danger but as deprivation.

Ray imagines Turtle as somehow like himself, provided he can be the kind of person who can see this sort of similarity ("maybe"). To call this "metaphorical thinking," then, is to suggest how, as Emmanuel Levinas forecasts, proximity to the other may yield an encounter with the face, or ethics, though the infinite presence of the other in Levinas's ethics gives way to a more unstable, contingent effect in Viramontes's novel.[27] In *Their Dogs*, ethics only takes hold when characters reach out across the breach of alterity with a figuration of similarity. If in Levinas the self is constituted by the ethical appeal of the other, in Viramontes, the self is transformed or at least made contingent by the

metaphorical approach to the other, a fragile, provisional form of encounter. We see this most clearly in the very first path-crossing between
Turtle and Tranquilina, an encounter that sets up and helps interpret
the novel's end, wherein physical escape has been foreclosed and love
appears doomed. At the beginning of the novel, Tranquilina and her
mother are rushing home through an unexpected rainstorm, carrying
a package of donated meat for their nightly missionary soup kitchen.
Nearby, Turtle considers jumping them for the package, which she
hopes includes food. Her plan is simply to "bump her and run with
the package. God-sent easy," but, in the instant before the attack, she
observes the intimacy between Tranquilina and her mother, and she
is stopped in her tracks when Tranquilina unaccountably "lift[s] her
arms and open[s] the wings of her poncho" and then flashes Turtle
a smile of "incredible delight" (28). The wing-like poncho and the
surprising smile save Tranquilina at this moment and translate into
instances of physical flight later in the novel, but here Turtle's letting-
be simply suggests she accepts the grace of the smile and that perhaps
she is even moved by the evident bond between Tranquilina and her
mother. The encounter is accompanied by the "clack" of thunder, a
sound that will be echoed by the "tock" of bones when Turtle meets
the homeless woman, a signal for when Turtle is dispossessed of her
ruthless persona.

Tranquilina's experience of the encounter, while startlingly different, likewise indicates how the neighborhood itself can reconstitute
her sense of self. Tranquilina has only recently relocated to East Los
Angeles, her birthplace, after being raped and beaten after a tent-
revival meeting in Texas. She and her mother are disoriented, as the
arrival of the freeways interrupts formerly well-known circuits, and
they are unsure how to get home. While adjusting the sleeves of her
poncho—not lifting wings—she spots Turtle—whom she perceives to
be a man—staring at her hungrily, and she stiffens in fear and dread of
another attack. Even more so than with Ray, Tranquilina knows that
Turtle's fearsome aspect originates in desperation, but still traumatized

by her rape, she feels only the immediate urge to escape. Her smile of "delight" is a forced attempt to mask her fear and to hearken the self who once believed without reservation. If something salvific occurs between Turtle and Tranquilina, it is not transcendental, not some force that originates outside the self, and its expression is an affirmation of Tranquilina's doubt and contingency, and not confirmation of her resolute faith. Or, to borrow from Rosi Braidoitti, Tranquilina's reconfiguration of the space between her and Turtle "is no Christian affirmation of life nor transcendental delegation of the meaning and value system to categories higher than the embodied self. On the contrary, it is the intelligence of radically immanent flesh that states with every single breath that the life in you is not marked by any signifier and it most certainly does not bear your name."[28]

Crucially, the *misperceptions* occurring during the encounter preempt the seemingly fated attack. For Viramontes, scenes of contingency and assemblage bear the possibility of a reality beyond the immediate situation, visible in the metaphor: Tranquilina contorted her face into the image of love, and Turtle saw an angel, and the encounter is structurally the same as the previously noted meeting of Turtle and the homeless woman.[29] Importantly, it is the characters themselves who "read" each other metaphorically: Turtle reads the poncho as wings and sees a harmony between mother and daughter that does not really exist, and like the Marian imagery described earlier, the metaphorical capacity of perception allows a way of reading otherwise, calling forth transformations and "worlds of becoming," originating in but not wholly determined by the neighborhood.[30] Though these instances of metaphorical perception are not miraculous in any normative sense, they suggest a logic of the miracle that the final section of this chapter will explore: miracle and metaphor are part and parcel of the social assemblage in which they occur and require a receptive audience. And indeed, it is the audience's readiness to believe that permits either the miracle or the metaphor to be seen. One thinks of the appearance of the Virgin Mary in the bark of a tree, drawing thousands of pilgrims in New Jersey, supplicants who declared the image a miracle, even after the Archdiocese claimed otherwise.[31] Absent from contestations of the miracle—in fact, the absence is the reason for the contestations—is any evident hand of a deity. The miracle is by definition an instance of the ordinarily impossible, and should God convincingly appear, everyone would know the fix is in—God can do anything. Absent the transcendent, then, the miracle, like the metaphor, relies upon a receptivity toward the impossible, a readiness to believe that hearkens if not heralds other worlds.

All the perceptive and misperceptive "reads" described thus far are transformative to some degree, and all radically alter the structure of the encounter. In each, a crime scene is refracted into multiple possibilities, and the subsequent crises for the characters involved are also instances of what Deleuze and Guattari call "deterritorialization" or counterclaims on the ethos of the neighborhood. Each instance—the finger raised to the lips, the offer of a job, and "smile of incredible delight"—effects a kind of escape for the characters involved, not from the neighborhood but from the situation governed by violence and want, permitting the characters a "lin[e] of flight" into an ecology not yet determined.[32]

The novel directly links this deterritorialization with the miraculous and extends the metaphorical reach of the "line of flight" with a literal referent. Shortly after the encounter with Turtle, Tranquilina is suddenly born upward above the clouds, where she feels the wingtips of passing geese brush by (34). The moment is startling, and as in several other instances of the supernatural in the novel, she is not entirely sure what is happening, or even if it *is* happening. Tranquilina quickly returns to earth, and her mother, who had been walking ahead seeking a way around the freeway onramp, notices nothing. For the reader, the flight presents the opposite problem of the ambiguous Marian metaphor mentioned before: the description is clear, Tranquilina is airborne, but the moment seems to have no consequence within the novel, no metaphorical clarity, accomplishing nothing. However, the short-circuited flight tells us something about the operation of miracles in the novel overall. Miracles occur as ruptures—both eruptions and interruptions, events that break from the spatial and material configurations of given life and from linear time. Tranquilina's flight is, by contrast, tethered to the city: she and her mother are trapped in the entombing landscape and caught within a temporal flow as they rush back home to prepare the soup to serve to the homeless. Tranquilina reflects on her parents' story of miraculous flight from Mexico, and rather than take her own flight as support for the story, she is unable to imagine either as possible. It is as if the miraculous flight, at least for the unreceptive and unprepared Tranquilina, never happened.

THE INSIDE OF THE THING AND THE THING ITSELF

All of the encounters described thus far are embedded in the neighborhood that Viramontes has painstakingly mapped for the reader. Across her fiction, the neighborhood figures as an overdetermined political and ethical space: playful neighborhood children become violent, friends hide from one another behind walls of mistrust, and proximity in general typically yields both intimacy and fear.[33] In *Their Dogs Came with Them*, as in most of Viramontes's fiction, the neighborhood is a contact zone where the conflicting imperatives of ethics, politics, and psychology can be paralyzing in any encounter. The neighbor thus becomes what Freud conjectured, a subject of both fear and uncanny similarity, and characters develop a "carapace" of paranoia that guards "against an even more disturbing attack from inside."[34] As Eric Santner has explained, the neighbor figures the psychical "excess" we all bear and that we all have no choice but to encounter in the other.[35] The neighbor, disturbingly strange like me, engages me with a lateral breadth—as I assemble a landscape of settled and competing interests—and an interior depth—as I contend with the psychical turbulence that I share with my neighbor.

In *Their Dogs*, a regime of laws, surveillance, violence, punishment, and dehumanizing missives outlining quarantine zones constitutes this paranoia. Characters are continually forced to recommit to defensive identities and to beat back internal crises resulting from fractured families and mental illness. Turtle's "carapace" is her leather jacket, shaved head, and bad-assed persona, signaling malevolence to the world around but more effectively containing and eventually suffocating the complex, vulnerable woman she has had to reject in order to survive. If the neighborhood is, as Kenneth Reinhard puts it, "a place, a subset, or element where there is no boundary, no difference, between the inside of the thing and the thing itself," where "the thing" is both psychologically composed and materially assembled, then Turtle's attempt at closing out the world and Tranquilina's desire to be open to it constitute the two aspects of neighborhood, material and metaphorical.[36] People are the neighborhood, even as the neighborhood presses on and alters the course of their lives. Neighborhoods function and stabilize when people living within them are assembled within an arrangement of sites and stories that add coherence to their lives. In *Their Dogs*, the neighborhood is destabilized not only through the imposition of artificial border lines in the form of freeway walls but also through a circumscription of the area as a zone of detention, a move that recasts all the area dwellers as suspect and subject to a law that is both outside of and constitutive of the neighborhood.

If this mutuality of the neighborhood is a source of paranoia, it may also explain how characters reassemble *and* reconfigure the neighborhood itself through acts of letting-be and generosity. The tense encounters described prompt characters to retrieve a version of themselves that resituates and locates them in the material space of the neighborhood—wherein they experience fear and danger—and in a more imaginary space of futurity, a neighborhood remade in Ray's case. In both instances, characters act not out of an embedded faith in the inherent goodness of others or the common kinship of all people but to save—or affirm the salvation of—their own lives. This, concludes Reinhard, among other recent theorists of "the neighbor," is the meaning of Leviticus's "Love thy neighbor as thyself," for which "*love* is the decision to create a new open set, to knot two interiorities into a new logic of world, a new *neighborhood.*"[37] This is neither romantic love nor the love of *agape,* nor is it a Christian *caritas,* because it is not a love that originates from or between individuals. Rather, it is a love that *produces* separation and "two-ness"—and thus the possibility of an ethics—by shattering the illusion of universality or a unified field. Returning to Thomas Claviez's elevation of metonymy over metaphor, and recalling Laclau's privilege of the same noted in the Introduction, we might say, following Reinhard, that *Their Dogs* reverses the prioritization of metonymy over metaphor. For Laclau, metonymy signals the material conditions that give rise to political activism, while metaphor signals something like hardening of a fluid activism into a static politics of identification. In *Their Dogs,* however, it is just the reverse: metaphor, the conduit of love, is what creates distinction and particularity, and permits the possibility of both an ethics of love and a politics of engagement that would follow. Where before characters perceived a flat, blank space, a backdrop of either enemies or saved souls, the neighborhood becomes a place where others are unassimilated to the self but remain distressingly proximate, altering the self's itinerary.

Through his paraphrase of philosopher Alain Badiou, Reinhard explains, "[L]ove is what 'fractures' that imaginary unity, brings out the universal truth of disjunction in a particular situation."[38] In the encounters described earlier, it is the static neighborhood itself that is fractured, and disjunction, the metaphorical crack in the sidewalk, is the site of love's emergence. Ethics for Badiou is the imperative to "never forget what you have encountered" and to live in the new "arrangements of [your] multiple being," or, in *Their Dogs,* remain committed to the reconstitution of the neighborhood that occurs through the encounter with the other.[39] The dissolution of the "carapace" or "shell" in Turtle's case trades static being for a process of becoming, or "becoming undone," as Elizabeth Grosz has put it.[40] In *Their Dogs Came with Them*, "becoming undone" occurs as characters quite literally remap the space of their neighborhood to account for its shifting boundaries, while engagements among neighbors either open up or close down circuits of transit and social exchange. The result is not the affirmation of the self *against* institutions, the common theme of protest literature. Rather, it is the release of the myth of the self itself—the dissolution of the "carapace" of paranoia and even the imaginary boundary lines that would distinguish people from their situatedness.

A brief but consequential instance of this dissolution occurs in *Their Dogs* when the teenager Ermila is rushing home to beat the city's curfew and is stopped at the roadblocks by a QA officer, Ulysses Rodriguez. The name is enough to resonate with the cartographical wanderings of James Joyce's characters, only, in *Their Dogs*, Ulysses stands for containment and constraint, rather than neighborly proximity. When Ermila complains about the slow line to have her identification checked, Ulysses accuses her of being a troublemaker and pulls her out of line for interrogation. Arrogating the power to control both space and time, he demands to know why she is out past curfew. Suddenly, however, a different order of time and space subsumes them both when she tells him that she was working late at her job at a used car lot—the same lot, it turns out, where Ulysses bought his own first car years ago. Awash in memory, Ulysses no longer polices the boundary line. Instead, he is briefly possessed by his dormant teenage memories and becomes the neighbor to Ermila, made proximate through their mutuality.[41] When he good-naturedly waves her through the barriers to her home, she surprisingly defers her free passage to another woman carrying a small, visibly ill child, an important act that blocks mutuality from becoming conspiracy.[42] Different from other moments when mutuality effects escape (for the homeless woman or Tranquilina), Ermila's choice to stay put is yet another "line of flight" insofar as it resists the reterritorialization of the boundary line and usurps the power of Ulysses to control who gets to cross it.

Ermila's decision to offer her free passage to another woman echoes an earlier dissolution of boundaries as part of the affirmation of the neighborhood. Ermila's bedroom window faces out onto First Street, where every morning she sees the laborers gathering at the bus stop or rushing to work and mutters toward the street, "You're fucked," a brutally sympathetic but finally distancing claim of separation, affirming the difference between home and street, her individuality versus their multitude. These border lines are breached eventually, as she comes to realize that she too has nothing but "fucked-up options" as a poor Latina, and she revises her daily affirmation to "We're fucked" (176, 193). If this identification seems all too fatalistic for the way it simply circumscribes Ermila within the circle of those who have poor options and live in deprivation, her subsequent affirmation of mutuality indicates a transformation not only within her but in the neighborhood she dwells in, through an act of love.

WE'RE NOT DOGS

Their Dogs Came with Them ends in a dark, dead-end alley, near the central bus station, where Ermila's cousin Nacho hopes to escape the pursuit of Turtle's gang. The setting and the killing at the end suggest the end of becoming, transformation, and even endurance, while fear, despair, and brutality are the overwhelming responses to space so heavily defended and policed. By the end, the reader bears the burden of sustaining the novel's prior hint that the neighborhood can nourish and not only destroy life. Turtle is on the scene, swept up by her gang before the sun rises and she can claim her new life. She is high on PCP, and when her gang leader hands her a screwdriver to deliver the killing blow, she suddenly feels "the dynamite rage of all the fucked-up boys stored in her rented body" (322). She stabs the screwdriver through Nacho and then thrusts a second time, "so deep through the pit of the boy's belly, it hit the brick wall and when she heard the snap-crack of bone, she took it to be the boy's rib and not her own wrist and arm bones breaking" (322). The awful crack of the wall against her own strength marks the sorrowful end to the transformative capacity of Turtle's letting-be. When she looks up from her victim, she discovers her gang has abandoned her, and as she stares at her fractured arm, she is startled by the sting of bullets: QA sharpshooters firing at the "undomesticated mammals" in the alley.

Also in the alley is Tranquilina, who is searching for the missing college student Ben and comes across the killing scene. The closing lines are overwhelmingly metaphorical, but the metaphors careen and collide against expectations, challenging us to read against the grain of the novel's action. Tranquilina holds Turtle's body in a pose recalling the *pieta*, a radical resignification of that image, as Turtle maintains the posture of the dead Jesus, with Tranquilina occupying Mary's role. That Turtle and Tranquilina are taken for dogs by the QA amplifies the grim foreclosure of the neighborhood and the end of transformative encounters, and seems to undercut the efficacy of the metaphorical pose: the reader may see it, but if they are still shot like dogs, so what? The constrained neighborhood and now the dead-end alley echo the earlier citation of Ray's childhood internment, and the dog-like status of the two women suggests they are the walking dead.[43] Dogs have roamed across the novel as the inhuman signs of neighborhood dysfunction and the excuse for governmentality and the ruling state of exception; however, Tranquilina's final words are a refusal to all the killers on the scene: "'*We'rrrre not doggggs!*' Tranquilina roared in the direction of the shooters" (324). At this point, the motif of the dog is both the sign for and the condition of abjection, and the assertion of human being within the idiom of the growl suggests that "the human being is . . . the *différance* inscribed within the inhuman force field that . . . she seeks to transcend and overcome."[44] Tranquilina's cry disfigures rather than "reconfigures" the stable terms of recognition, and paraphrasing Jacques Ranciére, the growl slashes "noise" through the audible human voice, resulting in a "shift" of her "body from a place assigned to it" to a new "destination."[45] But where is that destination?

And how can disfiguration instantiate something beyond the dead-end alley to renew transformation?

The narrative, including the closing lines, suggests there is some place beyond, namely the world of the reader, and that the act of reading itself requires the reconfiguration of possibility for Tranquilina. The novel's closing lines signal how reading may make metaphors happen and how metaphors may align with miraculous rupture:

> The sharpshooters steadied their barrels.
>
> Shoulders back, Tranquilina raised her chin higher, as Mama had told her time and again, to fill up with the embrace of ancestral spirits. Shouting voices ordered her not to move, stay immobile, but she lifted one foot forward, then another, refusing to halt. Two inches, four, six, eight, riding the currents of the wilding wind. Riding it beyond borders, past the cesarean scars of the earth, out to limitless space where everything was possible if she believed. (329)

The contingency of the novel's ending leaves the reader with two questions: does Tranquilina actually lift off the ground and fly away, or is she shot?[46] And what could "limitless space where everything [is] possible" mean? The phrase reads like a protean but formless metaphor that can only exist if the reader maintains faith that Tranquilina indeed "believed." If we believe she believes, we effect a bridge of mutuality between our world and the world of the text, and so sustain the possibility not only of her flight, but of possibility itself, some other form of life. Borrowing from Badiou, "it is a matter of showing how the space of the possible is larger than the one assigned—that something else is possible."[47] That is, the novel presses the reader to believe in some transformative space of the possible, even as the brutally real world of the novel forecloses that possibility.

Nothing stands as a figure to ground the suspended possibility of "if she believed" because, as the novel has previously hinted, belief itself is what produces figuration in the first place, making metaphors to figure a life we only dimly understand. Spivak explains, "the working of the trace resists figuration. . . . [T]he impulse of the 'human' is to turn the trace into sign."[48] Evincing traces is the commitment of literature, while seeking the trace in the figure—what we typically call interpretation, but aligned here with belief—is the work of reading.[49] The figure is what we produce out of the trace; the metaphor stands in for a real we barely sense and to which we do not know how to otherwise lay claim, and so figuration is evidence of our will to believe and not the object of belief itself. We are left as the ones who make the metaphor, not only out of the remnant possibility within the novel, but of our own human impulse to believe in becoming, "limitlessness," and "all things possible."

The miracle, too, may be evidence of a will to believe, and I close with a consideration of what it means for a reader to believe in Tranquilina's belief—what does that belief engender or make possible, and how might it live in the world beyond the text?[50] Thinking about the miracle's place in political theory, Bonnie Honig investigates Franz Rosenzweig's representation of the miracle as dialogic, involving both rupture *and* reception, a miracle-performing deity *and* a people desiring the miracle. Paraphrasing Rosenzweig, Honig explains, "[M]iracle is an ambiguous sign that thrusts upon humans the responsibility to receive and read it. That responsibility presupposes and requires a readiness and preparation that may be provided by community membership, liturgical practice, material preparation, and study."[51] The significance of a miracle is not only that it ruptures reality, but that it "follow[s] a certain arc: it was predicted, prophesied, and the event then occurred. Thus, on Rosenzweig's account, the event's character as a miracle is tethered to the event's function as a sign or portent of divine providence."[52] Honig goes on to read the story of Moses twice striking the rock in Exodus, in contradiction to God's command that he *tell* the rock to bring forth water. Moses' betrayal, Honig claims, was not of God but of the Israelites who were thirsting for prophecy, longing to interpret the divine into their world. They needed the water, but even more, they needed the words to bring forth the water. Here the similarities to the end of *Their Dogs* are startling: the double strike against the obdurate—the wall, the rock—closes down worlds of becoming, while human speech heralds the occasion for belief. The water can only be a miracle if it was anticipated, and Tranquilina's speech-act, roaring out against her dehumanization, places the onus on the reader to believe in and figure forth "limitless space, where all things are possible."

Can we believe that Tranquilina believes in her mission to love and care for her neighbors, even at their worst, and even amid the dehumanizing regime of quarantine and elimination? Surely the novel has made a reader bereft and vulnerable—like Turtle when she sees Tranquilina's "smile of incredible delight," like Ray when he recognizes Turtle's desperation—and so we rightly long for Tranquilina's salvation. Being ready to summon the miracle is the necessary precondition for the miracle's event, and the rupture of the miracle, if prophesied and accepted as such, may transform a reader's world, insofar as it amplifies and reconfigures the space of possibility. In this way, the novel's handoff of the triad of belief to the reader, carried on the conditional "if" for which the reader bears responsibility, makes the act of reading consequential. The reader participates in the dialectical rupture and becomes responsible for the emergence of the novel's "truth" (in Badiou's sense) into the world. We are the ones enjoined to "never forget what [we] have encountered": Turtle, marked for death, is also the blessed Virgin; Tranquilina, gunned down, is also the embodiment of resistance and possibility. It is in this sense that Badiou's conception of truth comes in to play: we are compelled to be faithful to the truth of the event of our own understanding, neither to misread reality nor to look away from a reality we hardly understand. Faithful to the "situation" of reading, we become a neighbor to the text, where there is no difference between the inside of the thing, the narrative, and the thing itself, the situation of reading. Reading means forming a neighborhood, just beyond the pages of the novel, the anticipated limitless

space of possibility. Believing in the miracle, the reader likewise makes
the metaphor and thereby bears responsibility for the novel. Though
beyond the scope of this discussion, I mean to suggest that a reader so
described would have to consider the very real neighborhood of East
Los Angeles, and other neighborhoods like it, and to consider that the
neighborhood provides the raw material for Viramontes's metaphors,
which themselves enable new ways of seeing the neighborhood, both
as it is and as it could be. Writing against the grain of urban renewal
and economic development, Viramontes nonetheless instructs us to
see how imaginative acts of love and care constitute the beginning and
not simply the ends of urban transformation.

Explaining her commitment to writing, Viramontes has said,
"[W]riting is the only way I know how to pray."[53] Perhaps she means
writing portends futurity (the next sentence, then the next . . .) and
imaginatively hearkens a community of readers who will decode if not
the meaning of the metaphor, the trace of a reality that the metaphor
can only hint at.[54]

NEGOTIATING SPACE

If writing is like prayer, what is the role of the reader for manifesting
that prayer in the world? Or to put it in more secular terms, how can
reading be a form of intervention—not simply taking an ethical stance,
which may accomplish nothing, but part of a process of engagement
with the material world? If, as Paula Moya argues in *The Social Imperative*, literature is "an important actor in the ongoing struggle to imagine . . . another way to be human and free," where do we find the relay
between reading and action, between imagination and reality?[55] This
chapter presumes that Viramontes's novel depends on just such a relay,
or better yet, a network between reader, text, and world, and Chapter
2, on the Watts Writers Workshop, goes even further to examine the
ethics and politics of navigating that network. There are ways of getting
it wrong—of confusing reading for acting, or writing for liberation, or

worse, representation for democracy itself—but in this chapter I began with the writer's faith (Viramontes's) and the reader's responsibility, and have explored how reality otherwise may become the reader's responsibility. I have examined *Their Dogs*'s gestures toward new possibilities, figured in metaphor, which necessarily emerge from and correspond to the material or metonymic circumstances of the novel's characters. The neighbor and the neighborhood constitute a structure for understanding the characters' social arrangements as well as a reader's potential for forming a network or neighborhood with the text. What remains to be seen is what happens in real-life neighborhoods in a city such as Los Angeles, and how the theory and practice of love of the neighbor gain purchase on the material conditions of people's lives.

In this final section, I turn to a real-world example of the neighbor that draws together several of the strands of politics and ethics discussed thus far. This chapter has raised questions about the possibility of a political response to state-based human and civil rights violations in Los Angeles, specifically those instances when law is instrumentalized so as to control or contain people, and in order to accelerate economic development that privileges some lives over others. What does real revolution look like in these circumstances, especially when the economic sea change that is the gentrification of low-income neighborhoods can initially strike some as the beginning of progress? As Walter Benjamin made clear in his timely essay, "Critique of Violence," the key question is how to organize a political response that does not become subsumed in either a law-preserving amelioration or a counter-hegemonic revolt that necessarily resolves into new forms of power and control, so that the destiny of the neighborhood is not routed into exclusionary rejection of the outside, but remains the "open set" forecast by Reinhard and others.[56] My hint, drawn from Viramontes, is that the neighbor figures a form of political efficacy *and* opens outward as an ethical stance that prevents it from being resolved. For Benjamin, the imperative to evade the traps of power and hegemony directs us to hear a "divine commandment," which does not necessarily mean the voice of God, but some directive that breaks from all intact regimes of power and control.[57] The neighbor likewise bears the structure of the miracle, insofar as neighbors and neighborhoods have to be anticipated and desired in order to exist, and their existence has the quality of an event, realigning the reality of one's and one's neighbor's lives.

Union de Vecinos, or UV, is the continuation of the work begun by a Catholic Parish Church in the housing projects in Boyle Heights in the late 1980s, though it now operates independently throughout the Boyle Heights neighborhood, in the very same space of the city represented in *Their Dogs Came with Them*.[58] Grounded in liberation theology, including Marxist principles, UV exists to empower residents of Boyle Heights to make active claims of communal ownership on their neighborhood. UV's motto echoes liberation theology's basic process for addressing poverty and injustice in local contexts, "see, reflect, act." In liberation theology, seeing involves being a witness to suffering, while witnessing includes understanding the legal, political, and economic underpinnings of suffering. Poverty happens for a reason, and liberation theology draws on Marxist analytical processes for assessing the holistic bases of localized poverty. Reflection involves seeking antecedents and comparisons between the present and the local with the historical and the biblical. On the premise that Jesus is an advocate for the poor and dispossessed, and that Catholicism is a program of social justice, UV reflection involves locating in textual sources an ethos and action plan to remedy suffering, increase health and safety, and secure broad, enduring justice. Reflection includes prayer, and it's important to recall both Viramontes's hint that writing is a form of prayer and the Latin root of prayer, *orare*, which denotes a formal mode of speaking, involving reason, as its English derivative, *oration*, makes clear. The UV community regards its practice of prayer to be a form of thinking through material conditions and possibilities for living otherwise. Acting as a community, UV takes pride and power in the conviction that it is following a mandate which supersedes and thus which might recalibrate localized politics.

Initially, parish-church-based organizing began in the housing projects in the late 1980s, when Boyle Heights was suffering from several interrelated social cataclysms that marked off and limited residents' access to the space of their own city, largely controlled by gangs and police. The population of residents without legal permission to be in the United States increased, including refugees from El Salvador, Guatemala, and Nicaragua, fleeing U.S.-backed civil wars. Between the extrajudicial street violence and lack of legal legitimacy among so many residents, Boyle Heights residents were often reluctant to speak out about impoverished schools; poor housing facilities; and their exposure to industrial pollution from nearby railyards, freeways, and manufacturing facilities. That is, the neighborhood did not know itself as neighborhood. Moreover, there was no public discourse linking faith practices and political practices. Indeed, in the 1980s there were comparatively few political practices. Neighbors lived in fear of gangs: drug sales, drive-by shootings, muggings and other forms of assault, vandalism, and random violence not only dominated the neighborhoods but kept individual families indoors and in fear. In this way, there was no "neighborhood" per se, as all territory was contested by gangs and police, and residents retreated from public space in order to avoid being conscripted (or worse). To the extent that families sought to protect themselves they conceded the public sphere as a site of violence, and so did not participate as agents in that sphere.

Upon its founding in 1996, *Union de Vecinos* focused on the fight for low-income housing options in Boyle Heights, and soon became leaders for antipoverty, social justice transformation in the area. UV is lead by a small team of planners, including its co-director, Leonardo Vilchis, with whom I've spoken at length over several visits to Boyle Heights. Besides the co-directors, who persist through the support of small grants and fundraising efforts, UV is effectively organized and run by "*coordinadores de vecindario*" or neighborhood coordinators—people who have studied with UV leaders and have taken charge of their own particular apartment block, corner, or alleyway. As is typical

with these sorts of organizations, the process of organization on behalf
of neighborhoods helps form the desired outcome itself, as neighbors
communicate and collaborate on the common project of envisioning
a better world in their midst. Coordinators form committees, which
identify particular needs of their locality, typically including access
to health care and fresh, healthy food, pedestrian safety, and above
all, safe streets free from gang and police violence. Local actions are
at once modest and extraordinarily successful. Among the most bold
moves, and the first step on a long road, was for UV to get to know the
gangs. The group asked simply, who is in a gang? And what do these
people want, fear, and hope for? There is a moment in *Their Dogs* when
Turtle is having a face-off with another person on the street, and the
man responds to Turtle's malevolence with the caring query, "What's
your problem, *carnal?*", a disarming question that Turtle takes to be
an expression of genuine concern. For UV, this sort of direct engagement with the gangs is sourced in the church-based ethos of loving the
neighbor, with love requiring familiarity. An early event, which some
residents describe as a turning point for the neighborhood, involved
hosting a back-alley cookout, and inviting the gang members to participate. It is hard to overstate just how terrified residents were of the
gangs, and how courageous this effort was. Though gang members
were invited to the cookout, and mingled just beyond the alley, none
would actually come in and join the residents. The residents, in turn,
took it upon themselves to make plates of food and bring them to
the gangs. Women volunteered to carry the food, as a man's approach
was considered likely to be met with a violent reaction. This halting,
tentative arrangement became the subject of that weekend's Sunday
sermon at the local church, and residents who attended church recognized themselves in stories of Jesus feeding his followers. So fortified,
they built upon the initial event with subsequent cookouts, each time
strengthening a rapport with gang members, to the point at which
they could make claims on the territory. Those claims were simple:
"We live here, too," residents and captains told the gangs. "We, too,

live on this block, dwell in these alleys. Our children can play on these streets, and we will be part of this neighborhood." UV members tell me that the gang members are remarkably shy, wholly without social skills, and often adverse to social confrontations unrelated to their programmatic violence. As residents increasingly established their public presence, gangs retreated, not wanting to engage.

This sort of occupation of the neighborhood redraws its borders, potentially converting them from boundary lines limiting access to more fluid spaces of inclusion. If before, the principle markings of the neighborhood were the graffiti tags painted by gang members in order to mark off spaces of identification and prohibition, the UV actions repopulated the neighborhood, as its members made claims on space, and remapped the neighborhood in the image of the neighbor. A similar tactic involved what UV members described as "love walks," during which large groups of people lit candles and walked slowly through their area streets after dark—a typically unthinkable activity prior to UV. The idea for "love walks" arose from bible-study sessions in which UV residents considered the model of Jesus, walking on the surface of the water in the Galilee, a miraculous event, but one which they felt they could replicate. For UV, walking at night in what was previously known gang territory was the equivalent of a miracle.

Union de Vecinos's engagement with liberation theology illustrates the process by which metaphor meets miracle described in the preceding discussion of *Their Dogs Came with Them*. More than simply reading the bible for allegories of divine instruction on how to deal with material problems, UV activists "read" their material reality already through the filter of theology, insofar as their comprehension of justice came directly from a Marxist-informed reading of the bible. The three-part process of "see, reflect, act" does not in fact assume separate domains of the secular world and the sacred text, or material analysis and religious judgment. Rather, as Leonardo described it to me, it's something like a felicitous "hermeneutical circle," in which material and textual analyses are mutual, incessantly informing one another. Though I do not wish to minimize the importance of the divine to those practicing liberation theology, my interest in *Union de Vecinos* is not based in a shared religiosity. Rather, the interest is in the process by which world and text become co-constitutive. As with the prior discussion of miracle in Viramontes's novel, liberation theology's miracle originates not in the divine other but in the receptivity to radical possibility among the neighbors themselves. That possibility is woven into neighbors' assessment of their situation, which imagines justice precisely through its analysis of injustice. Leonardo insists that the analytical work involved in imagining otherwise constitutes "hope," which is not a passive or fantastical regard of the future, but a production of the future in the consciousness of the present. Here the promise of other worlds is bound up with the material world itself, as the idea latent within it, something that can be seen precisely through a deep understanding of the causes and consequences of injustice.

In her account of liberation theology, Kristien Justaert proposes "interconnection and entanglement, rather than transcendence, as the basis for liberation theology's method," in which there is no distinction between world and text, or the secular subject and the sacred subject.[59] Rather, sacred and secular, material experience and theological reflection are entangled in a single, multiply composed subject. Put more simply, the poor know they are poor, they know why it is wrong, and through collective analysis they can envision broad-scale remedies. Biblical hermeneutics are the means for discovering the broadest possible account of justice, and the faith to act as if the miracles were possible. Justaert argues that it is "the cry of the body . . . that should be the starting point for liberation theology," matching the promise of metaphor in Viramontes's novel.[60] The point is that the metaphor—which thus far has been congruent with the miracle, the event of love, and even the face of the other, in Levinas's terms—is entangled with metonymical or material relations—the conditions of injustice assessed through the lens of miracle's possibility. Crossing the street with a carton of food for a clutch of gang members who are staring at you may require faith in the divine, but that faith is felt in the body, which may simultaneously shake with fear even as confident legs carry it forward.

Subsequently, UV organized nonviolent, participatory, and inclusive claims on space. Cleaning the alleys, disposing of trash, finding out who makes the alleys dirty—and why—and speaking directly to those people. Over time, several neighborhood alleys have been converted from trash dumps and sites for drug dealing into far more imaginative, inclusive, if still outlaw places. Some alleys have been painted over to look like swimming pools or beach scenes, and other alleys have been fitted with canopy poles to accommodate weekend farmers markets. Neither these markets, nor any of the interventions described have been sanctioned or legally permitted, from the retrofitting to the painting to the roadblocks. This sort of reorganization of space recalls and amplifies the brief moment when Ermila and the QA officer Ulysses recompose the neighborhood roadblock into a shared space of communal memory, and it is as if the alleyways are the rejoinder to Ermila's lament of limited, "fucked-up options," the possible otherwise to Nacho's, Turtle's, and Tranquilina's dead-end death. Gang members still congregate in this area, though they don't

FIGURE 1.1 *Union de Vecinos* bench with graffiti. Photo by Dean Franco.

like being part of large, nongang crowds and typically move on when other neighbors visit. As is clear in Figure 1.1, the gangs still tag the space, but with a surprising degree of discretion, and their tag co-exists with rather than overcomes the bright colors of the bench and the prominence of UV's own "tag."

On Friday nights, some residents have taken to blocking off the alleys with their own makeshift barriers, and then projecting family-friendly films on the walls. Residents make food, bring chairs and blankets, and settle in for a few hours outdoors. At one point during the first such occasion, a gang member pulled up to the alley entrance with his car and insisted that he had to pass through. He was rebuffed by the other residents, and told that he would have to wait till the movie ended. An odd standoff ensued, with the gangster sitting on the hood of his car, staring down the movie-watching residents, who simply returned to their chairs to watch the film. Eventually, the gangster left his car and sat down to watch with the residents, and has returned with his own chair for future movie nights.

In a conversation with Michel Foucault, Gilles Deleuze observed, "No theory can develop without eventually encountering a wall, and practice is necessary for piercing this wall."[61] *Union de Vecinos*'s work is such a practice, not piercing the wall but resignifying it as a borderline and not a boundary. While walking through one alley with Leonardo, I observed with some distress that a lovely mural, which had been painted

FIGURE 1.2 Alley wall in Boyle Heights. Photo by Dean Franco.

on a wall by residents of the adjacent apartment complex, had been tagged (Figure 1.2). A UV resident had painted a fantastic slogan, an innovative combination of Heidegger and Marx, "*La Vivienda es una Derecho Humano*" [Dwelling Is a Human Right]. A gang had tagged the mural however, and I expressed my distress to Leonardo.

"Notice," he said, "where the tag is placed." The gangs hadn't altered the claim for rights, and possibly, they had even honored it both by leaving the claim legible, and by effectively ratifying it with their own tag. Between the mural and the tag, Leonardo concluded, "We're negotiating space." Or, in the terms I've been using here, they are making a neighborhood.

CHAPTER 2

THE MATTER OF
THE NEIGHBOR
AND THE PROPERTY
OF "UNMITIGATED
BLACKNESS"

"Black optimism and Afro pessimism are asymptotic. Which one is
the curve and which one is the line? . . . It doesn't matter. . . ."

Fred Moten, "Blackness and Nothingness"[1]

THE CONTEMPORARY PHRASE "black lives matter"
insists on the materiality of racism by emphasizing black people's precarity before the law. More than a prompt for a "national conversation
about race," the phrase forces us to consider racial substance itself—how
the matter of blackness is manifest through violence and its afterlife as
public spectacle, and how attention to the material dimensions of racial
violence requires a new politics of black materiality. The power of the
phrase has been striking for its ability to rally community and to locate a
field of political engagement in which black activists are agents, controlling and not controlled by the prevailing discourse. Since the founding
of the United States, the capture and control of black bodies has always
been a violation of constitutional principles and declarations of rights,
and law has always had to wrap itself around and thereby sequester its
original crime. Or as Keeanga-Yamahtta Taylor puts it, "the distance
from the end of the Civil War, with the birth of Black citizenship and
civil rights, to the state-sanctioned beating and torture of Freddie Gray

constitutes the gap between formal equality before the law and the self-determination and self-possession inherent in actual freedom—the right to be free from oppression, the right to make determinations about your life free from duress, coercion or the threat of harm."[2] In this way, the phrase "black lives matter" and the attendant activism understand our present institutions of law and justice as tools of white supremacist racism over and above forces of liberation.

This power of the phrase is belied by its seeming simplicity, and it is striking to hear three common words get stuck in the throat. When white people say "black lives matter," they admit that heretofore white lives mattered more, and that being white has required the vulnerability of black people, including a raft of policies and tactics for constraining black freedom. "Black lives matter," therefore, does not simply displace whiteness from the rhetorical scene (in other words, "black lives matter, white lives don't"), it intends to initiate a new democracy of materiality in which political freedom is based not in liberal opportunity but on material redress.[3] Not exactly a performative speech act, as defined by J. L. Austin and others, in which iteration equals action, the statement is first an admission of inequality before the law, and second, a reinscription of radical (if not foundational) democratic premises within the material experience of blackness, rather than an elision of those experiences.[4] Those two dimensions, housed in the iteration of racial materialism, first signify that race has been made to matter for the purposes of exploitation—labor extraction, chiefly, but also for the purposes within the wider libidinal economy. And second, rather than saying, "Fine, let's do away with race," "black lives matter" means that redress can only occur by making racial boundaries more and not less visible.

The contemporary reactionary panic over any discursive attention to racism, banished as so much political correctness, suggests that talking about race does indeed matter, so much so that it threatens major institutions, including the university itself. Academia since the 1970s is particularly invested in discursive modes of racial remedy, and a very basic premise of academic multiculturalism, and especially of multicultural literature study, is that histories, geographies, and narrative and poetic accounts of the lives of racially subordinated people have the power to change that subordination.[5] But how? How does one cross the border between words and action? The question is central to taking on racism since, on the one hand we no longer believe in the biological substance of race, and on the other hand, we are enjoined to recognize that racialization is neither a mere optics ("I don't see race,") nor the effect of language (and thus dismissed as political correctness). Chapter 1 considered the efficacy of literature in the material world, arguing for the transformative capacities of metaphor—a vehicle for identification—in cooperation with metonymy—a vehicle for location. That chapter is about how reading literature can produce the conditions for material change, and how political activism draws on imaginative resources of storytelling and figurative mapping to make claims on space. In this chapter I shift the emphasis back to metonymy, or the geographical and social location of identity as the grounds for imagining otherwise. If, with Viramontes's novel, metaphor could be transformative precisely because it bridged over social location and geography, here I examine the priority of materiality and political identification as the basis of ethics, and not as the object of ethics' obviation.

As I have tried to indicate, the universalizing language that is the basis of our democracy—*all lives matter*—is part and parcel of a system of denigration and dispossession that sustains fictions of equality serving some in this country while disallowing others. Words block equitable polity. What is true in a phrase is at least as true in specific circumstances wherein we live, and we recall that the Black Lives Matter collective is tethered to black dispossession and precarity in specific locales: Brooklyn, Baltimore, Ferguson.[6] Los Angeles in particular illustrates how a city affords affluent, predominately white residents opportunity not simply *instead* of to others, but through the dispossession of others. The freeway, a motif in so much L.A. literature, and

a recurring theme in this book, accelerates labor-flow and capital increase at the same time that it exists to constrain and depress the value
of the lives of the city's black, brown, and poor.[7] This is the point of
Ermila's lucid if depressive exclamation, "We're fucked," as she looks
out the window to see not the continuation of a neighborhood that
was present in her early childhood but a freeway barrier wall, cir-
cumscribing her neighbor-space and her life's opportunities. All lives
matter, all have access to ride Los Angeles's freeways, but the freeways
were built as an active dispossession of some for the favor of others.
This is why, as Joshua Clover explains, recent rioters in Oakland and
elsewhere blocked freeways: "[T]he blocking of traffic, the interruption of circulation as an immediate and concrete project, registered
nothing so much as the unquenchable desire to *make it all stop*."[8] The
materiality of "matter" is already fractured by inequivalence, already
a site of vulnerability, and platitudes of equality are reinscriptions of
the violence to which poor and black and brown are already subject.

Elizabeth Povinelli's account of endurance is helpful at this stage
for thinking through how a claim for human worth, passed through
the charged term *matter*, can signal the workings of biopolitical gov-
ernance and dispossession, and the will to survive that dispossession—
a will that necessarily becomes political as it passes into discourse.[9]
Writing on Charles Burnett's 1978 film *Killer of Sheep*, about Watts
in the 1970s, Povinelli focuses on the endurance of the film's subjects
amid depressive, exhausting housing and labor conditions. 1970s-era
Watts was much like it was in the 1960s, which I detail further on:
impoverished, with run-down housing, few good jobs, and oppressive
policing. The film and Povinelli's treatment of it, however, focus less
on the regimes of control and more on the life force of the film's subjects, as they exist somewhere between endurance and exhaustion, to
use Povinelli's key terms. In the face of daily misery, it can be hard to
narrate the particularity of suffering, to name who is causing the suffering of a resident of Watts, say, and the usual gestures of theory may
likewise be too generalizing to pinpoint how misery and persistence

become mutually entwined as the ordinariness of a life.[10] In any case, free choice and self-determination, the hallmarks of liberalism, along with any manner of self-improvement projects, give way to what Povinelli calls "immanent obligations," the immediate, forced choices one has to make between food and rent. Budd Schulberg, founder of the Watts Writers Workshop (1965–1973), implicitly understood this situation, and assumed that his own obligation was shared by at least some of the residents of Watts. That conviction, that writing is not a choice but an obligation and part of the endurance of racist deprivation, would be the impetus for the Workshop, even as or especially as it transformed into a broader neighborhood project.

FROM BEVERLY HILLS TO WATTS

I investigate the Watts Writers Workshop's attempt to respond to social inequality with literary writing in order to further explore the interlocking of ethical and political practices, and of textual and material spaces. Operating amidst the Black Arts Movement, the Workshop's rise and fall suggests the narrow space between radical nationalist refusals of polity on the one hand and liberal handwringing—quietist claims of surprise and concern that achieve little or nothing—on the other. This is the space wherein the Workshop was founded and functioned, and it was the meeting ground for Budd Schulberg's vaguely formed but deeply felt desire for political redress of the material realities of racialized inequity in Watts. I focus on Schulberg, a border-crossing, wealthy, white Jewish writer from Beverly Hills who spent several years working in Watts, in order to trace how his earnest faith in representation was inevitably challenged by the more complicated dynamics of law and property that gave rise to the Watts Rebellion in the first place. In other words, I am interested in the point at which language meets material space. Schulberg was not naive, but neither did he anticipate how a writing project initiated to transcend place would inevitably enmesh him more deeply into that place. Attempting a universal ethics of the neighbor, predicated on an open "love," Schulberg ended up the political neighbor to Watts instead, which required more than, or at least a very different and unanticipated sort of, love. Trying to understand that shift and its implications for a politics of acknowledgment and redress is the point of this chapter.

It is to Schulberg's credit that he took on the spatial, geographical challenges of being a neighbor to Watts, though his work during that period betrays his nearly constant struggle to locate himself alongside the dispossessed and racially subordinate among whom he worked. Further on, I will pivot to James Baldwin, who interrogated Schulberg's presumptions about race and place and argued that L.A.'s segregated neighborhoods required the constant production of racial difference—black and brown as the enemy at the gate—in order to sustain myths of opportunity in a real-estate-driven economy. Turning to Baldwin helps in exploring the contours of Schulberg's understanding of the politics of black materiality in Watts, and suggests the spatial nature of the contemporary discourse of Black Lives Matter. Then and now, liberal presumptions about property rights and material increase are sustained by and in fact constitute racial sequestration and dispossession.

The Watts Writers Workshop was conceived as a resource for writers to transcend the neighborhood, and as a means of transmitting Watts stories beyond the city. Between 1965 and 1973, the Workshop recruited hundreds of black and Latino residents in the Watts and South Central districts, and a core group of writers published the Workshop anthology *From the Ashes: Voices of Watts* (1967).[11] Some writers went on to write plays for theater and film and television screenplays, and writer Johnnie Scott testified before a Congressional commission on government operations. According to Daniel Widener, "[B]y 1968, at least five workshop participants were regularly writing for three local television studios. Others had secured fellowships at Stanford, the University of Iowa, and the University of Ghana. Workshop alumni held teaching positions at the Ohio State University, George Washington

University, and at two local state university campuses in California."[12] Though initially eschewing the social and political programs operated by the Black Panthers—even while sharing space with the Panthers and their affiliates—Schulberg, too, was forced to confront the daily violence and dispossession experienced by writers—notably, routine arrests and harassment of workship participants by police—and so discovered that a literary project was first and foremost about securing stability, including property. After observing Workshop participants who were hungry, homeless, and harassed by police, Schulberg concluded that the Workshop needed a space, not to mention a legitimate street address to give to police during routine shakedowns, where its most indigent writers could retreat and write. The Workshop's most visible accomplishment was the establishment of Frederick Douglass House, a theater, writing, and meeting space for writers and performers. Formally opened in 1970, FDH succeeded all too well, housing and hosting a diverse range of black artists, writers, and performers, and garnering the attention of the FBI in the process. The Bureau installed an informant and agitator, who sabotaged the Workshop and eventually burned down Frederick Douglass House in 1973.[13]

The arson marked the end of a brief cultural renaissance in Watts. By the early 1970s, the Black Panther Party and its rival US Organization were crippled by internecine violence and FBI interference, and even the Black Arts scene, of which the Workshop was briefly a part, had atomized, its most well-regarded members becoming less identified with a political program and more with the centrifugal influences of contemporary art. Now, Frederick Douglass House and the Watts Writers Workshop appear mostly as footnotes, if at all, in literary histories and in discussions of African American and L.A. writing. Measured in terms of output or canonicity, the Workshop contributes little to literary history. However, for a study of the meeting grounds of social activism, writing, and the city, the Workshop's rise and fall suggests how writing is preceded and exceeded by the economic and geographic forces it would aim to represent.

Given the brevity of the Workshop's duration and its failure to log lasting results, it is surprising that Budd Schulberg spoke about the Workshop and Douglass House as among his proudest achievements. The author of hundreds of essays, several novels and biographies, and many screenplays, including the Academy Award–winning *On The Waterfront*, Schulberg would regularly speak about the Workshop until his death in 2009. Different from his previous work, including the novels *What Makes Sammy Run* (1941), *The Harder They Fall* (1947), and *The Disenchanted* (1950), which still hold up as insightful commentary on writing, fame, and self-destruction, the Workshop yielded almost no writing that anyone reads today, while *On the Waterfront* (1954) and *A Face in the Crowd* (1957) are Hollywood classics.[14] Prior to Watts, Schulberg had flirted with communism, and though he testified as a friendly witness for HUAC in 1952, he sidestepped the ideological about-face of so many of his peers, either into an all-American liberalism (notably, Elia Kazan, but also Irving Howe), or to neoconservativism. Indeed, Schulberg disparaged ideological loyalty, and had no patience for theories and systems. There were enough phonies to be exposed and brought down, and there was enough extant injustice to lament and correct, without having to reify new regimes of truth and correctness.[15] Rather, throughout his life Schulberg remained a fierce critic of economic inequality, racism, housing discrimination, and disparities in educational opportunities. He campaigned against redlining and racial covenants in California, and maintained a friendship with Bobby Kennedy, whom he subsequently advised on the need for radical solutions to racism and race-based social inequalities only days before the presidential candidate's assassination in 1968. For these reasons, it remains at once surprising and yet obvious that the peripatetic writer Schulberg, who lived in Los Angeles, New York, Boston, and Mexico, and who frequently traveled the globe in search of places to write and stories to tell, found the apotheosis of his commitments and the logical expression of his moral and political credo in a relatively small, highly localized writing project in Watts.

Though news stories typically pin the beginning of the Watts riots on the out-of-control arrest of a drunk driver, and the subsequent citizen outrage over his rough handling, black people's anger had been growing for many years, as the district was long shunted from the expanding prosperity of Los Angeles at large.[16] A former rail-line city south of downtown, Watts was incorporated into Los Angeles in 1926 and remained a working class, mixed-race neighborhood prior to World War II. During the war, as African Americans moved from the South and the Midwest to Los Angeles to work in wartime manufacturing, white citizens of Watts and the surrounding areas revolted, burning crosses, blowing up buildings, and generally terrorizing black citizens.[17] Because of the abundance of available land to the south and the west where white workers migrated, the unstoppable draw of manufacturing jobs, and persistent racial redlining, by the 1960s Watts was nearly all black. In the 1960s, education and health care facilities were substandard, and the building of freeways carved up and effectively cordoned off the greater South Central L.A. district from downtown and the Westside, further depressing real estate mobility.[18]

For years, residents of Watts had protested police harassment, substandard health and education institutions, widespread redlining practices, and their lack of representation on the city council. The decades-long collusion of city and state officials, realtors and lenders, city patriarchs, and land developers had rendered L.A. neighborhoods for the large part racially and ethnically homogenous, which made it easy to ignore the demands of a particular neighborhood or district without political power.[19] In 1964, California voters passed Proposition 14, a ballot initiative that effectively negated the Rumford Fair Housing Act, passed by the legislature the year before. Prop 14 simply stated that property owners were free to sell or rent to whomever they chose, an obvious opening for housing discrimination and a clear violation of federal law, and which was ruled unconstitutional in 1966. The debate over the initiative made national headlines and caused legislative furor, as the state GOP campaigned for it and the state governor, Pat Brown, warned against it. The terms of the debate were clear, and those opposing it were adamant that it was a retread of the same segregationist practices that were at the core of California real estate policy, and which were responsible for perpetuating the misery of neighborhoods like Watts. In 1964 and 1965, black and brown residents of Watts and other low-income neighborhoods understood that white voters had specifically aimed to sustain racial segregation neighborhood by neighborhood, and in 1965 Watts residents knew exactly what the riot was about, even as it struck white Angelenos as an eruption without precedent.

Schulberg expressed the sense many had that a part of the city had ruptured forth from its boundaries, as he watched the revolt unfold on the television screen in his living room. This geographical dislocation—Watts coming into contact with Beverly Hills—would subsequently determine the *spatial* nature of the Watts Writers Workshop, with the author further cutting across boundaries by visiting Watts the week after the revolt, and then through a series of maneuvers and initiatives as he attempted to carve out a space for himself and his writers.[20] That the Workshop could be destroyed not through an attack on any one person or even through counter-ideological writing but through real estate sabotage suggests how it was more than a liberal adventure; it was also something like a geography project, an attempt to link Beverly Hills and Watts.[21] Writing about that impossible geography in 1972, James Baldwin simply stated, "[T]hese two worlds would never meet, and that fact prefigured disaster for my countrymen, and me."[22] This was Baldwin's conclusion, even though he was friends with Schulberg and knew about the Workshop, and it seems like a bookend to Schulberg's own optimistic attempt to bridge the two worlds with a drive down the freeway.

For Schulberg, the freeway drive from Beverly Hills to Watts gave the illusion of connection even as it hardened boundaries across the city. The line he would trace across the freeway was also the border of division. This is because the freeways are agencies for the reinscription of the status quo of the city, as drivers merge with the boundaries and trace zones of inclusion and exclusion, passing over but not through a hundred different neighborhoods. As Henri Lefebvre puts it, "[T]he driver is concerned only with steering himself to his destination, and in looking about sees only what he needs to see for that purpose. . . . Thus space appears solely in its reduced forms. *Volume* leaves the field to *surface*."[23] If, as in Chapter 1, becoming neighbor meant dissolving the "carapace" of paranoia to permit boundless love, following Lefebvre we might consider the "car-apace" or freeway transit as the tracing of the violent negation of the other.[24] In the weeks after first coming to Watts, and then for years after—in newspaper op-eds, magazine articles, and the introduction to the Workshop anthology—Schulberg would write about the primal experience of driving from Beverly Hills to the ruins of Watts, indicating how writing in and about Watts was as much a geographical as a literary project, a remapping of his psychical understanding of the city. In an early draft, Schulberg described his transit this way: "[O]ut of the lush, plush, white, bright Beverly Hills I drove to the Santa Monica Freeway and breezed along . . . to the Harbor Freeway and turned off on Century Blvd.—running East past Broadway—Main Street—Alameda—Avalon—Central."[25]

Naming the streets is typically Angeleno, as every L.A. driver recognizes the off-ramps and overpass signs, and it would seem that Schulberg is calling attention to the act of actually exiting the freeway where white drivers rarely do.[26] As is the case now, when residents of L.A.'s recently gentrified downtown district trace a line across Compton on the way to the airport, for most, it's as if Compton never existed, though the reverse cannot be said for residents of Compton, who live with the noise and air pollution, the depressed property values and civic isolation brought by the freeways. Exiting at Watts marks Schulberg's line of flight, a departure from a spatial grid that exists to detour white, wealthy Angelenos around zones of economic deprivation. More to the point, the departure would engender a whole series of remappings of urban space, where a plane of metaphorical identities sustaining a white supremacist Los Angeles gives way to a more voluminous mapping of the distribution of resources through power.[27]

Being black in Watts in 1965 meant being poor; paying too high a rent for substandard housing; surviving the absence of social and civil services, including health care and adequate education; and being constantly subject to police harassment. This is the material reality that Schulberg confronted when he arrived in Watts, and the story he tells about his orientation is admirably one of awakening to his ignorance as well as a shift from a faith in "the word" to a commitment to place. He thought his workshop would simply involve training residents to write about place, but he discovered that the conditions of the place determined the possibility of writing. It wasn't a matter of writing *about* Watts, it was a matter of enduring Watts in order to write. And if initially he was chiefly concerned with the very fact of his own arrival—*look at me, I'm driving to Watts!*—he used his introduction to the Workshop anthology to demonstrate that the social production of space is the social production of race. A workshop that would help writers represent civic, structural racism would have to be as much a space-making venture as it would be an exercise in expression.

The theme of Schulberg's introduction, then, is self-effacement and displacement, as the author accounts for the erosion of his pretensions through a series of dislocating experiences, beginning with the drafting of the introduction itself. Writing in pencil on a yellow legal pad, Schulberg began, "I am sitting here right now in the Watts Happening Coffee House at 19802 Beach street, trying to write this from the inside out," with "Beach street" hastily crossed out, and the correct address, 103rd Street, added.[28] It's easy to imagine Schulberg jumping up from his chair to see just where he was, an epigrammatic instance of his disorientation interrupting and conditioning his writing. He continues in this vein, describing a group of young black men who are nearby watching TV when a commercial comes on advertising "the opportunity to get in on the ground floor of a new real estate

developer's dream." The commercial's pitch for golf courses and swimming pools, "within reach [says the commercial] of even the budget-
minded homemaker," makes Schulberg "squirm," but the men claim
the moment with their own ironical play on the commercial: "Shi-iit,
man!, I think I'll buy me two of' em, one f' my white maid," an in-
version that deftly comments on the unstated but clearly telegraphed
racialist pretensions of the planned community.²⁹ Finally, Schulberg
describes his misguided efforts to impress residents of the efficacy of
art by screening for them his most famous film, *On the Waterfront*,
only to discover that there is no movie theater in Watts. When he ar-
ranges a screening at a local community center, the film is interrupted
by a wailing woman at the mortuary across the street, crying for her
child who died of a fever. The film viewers run outside, and Schulberg
realizes that the residents of Watts did not need to be impressed by
the dramatic or cathartic powers of film—the story they were living
would continually interrupt the stories Schulberg and others wished
to show them, a lesson that "burn[ed]" in Schulberg's mind, a perhaps unconscious indication of how the young child's death by fever
marked Schulberg's writing.³⁰

The confusion, the squirming, and the burning suggest an affective and embodied reorientation for Schulberg. More than simply
expressing his emotional reaction to the deprivation of Watts, Schulberg's language suggests how his experiences dispossessed him of his
presumptions, and that the secure perspectives of a West L.A. writer
would give way to, and necessarily become harnessed by, the specific
material needs of Watts residents. The disruption of the film screening is particularly telling, as it effectively shifts priority from Schulberg's role as the master writer to the residents themselves. It is worth
recalling that Schulberg, who wrote the original story and then the
screenplay for *On the Waterfront*, was by then an established writer,
with substantial resources and a network of contacts (his father was
the head of what would eventually become Paramount Studios, and
the film's director, Elia Kazan, was a friend and frequent collaborator).

His film, about a union longshoreman desperately seeking the purity of the labor market, is displaced by a scene in which there is no market at all, where surplus labor is sequestered, policed, and allowed to die, yielding a scene of immiseration that would not submit to any heroic narrative template Schulberg might have brought with him. Stung by the experience, Schulberg confesses,

It had been naive and callow to think that I could go to Watts for three hours of a single afternoon once a week. A creative writing class in Watts was fine, as far as it went, but it didn't go very far for writers who were homeless, who had to pawn typewriters, who fainted from hunger in class. Most of these writers would fall apart because they had no address, no base, no center, no anchor. That discovery was the genesis of Douglass House.[31]

I will document Schulberg's efforts to secure funding and build Douglass House, and thereby account for his shift from writer to builder, but first I turn to the writers themselves, whose work, published in *From the Ashes*, testifies to the insecurity of place that characterized living in Watts. Schulberg came around to what his writers already knew: Watts was a ghetto, the residents of which could afford neither to leave nor to remain, and many of them wrote directly about their experience with housing, health care, and police harassment.[32]

Like most black residents of Watts, the majority of the Workshop writers or their parents were born outside of California, with many families migrating from Texas and the Midwest to pursue wartime industrial work. Not surprisingly then, many of the Workshop participants wrote about their relationship to property in general and Watts in particular. *From the Ashes* includes poems, stories, and essays that pinpoint the experience of poverty in Watts, and narrate the feeling of being trapped, as if on an island in the heart of Los Angeles. Johnnie Scott, who published an essay in *Harpers* and went on to earn an MFA degree in creative writing, described living in the Watts tenement, Jordan Downs, where at night the floors were covered with cockroaches, a "shifting blackness in the blackness," explaining, "in time man learns to adjust to anything, anyone, any fear" (98). Another instance of dispiriting autocartography is Jeanne Taylor's story, "The House on Mettler Street," which gives a precise street address, catalogs the house's dingy, depressive features, and concludes "enough, of the house on Mettler street!" (73). The "enough" is an especially sorrowful expression, as the narrator has no hope of leaving the very space she can no longer stand to live in. Scott, Taylor, and others published in the anthology are localizing their misery, while linking it to the human experiences of depression, frustration, and survival. Different from the usual outside-in point of view provided by national media, which assigns a general misery to an entire place, this sort of street-address localizing attaches the particular experiences to individual people, giving frustration and anger an origin, and rebellion a cause.

Sonora McKellar's essay, "Watts—The Little Rome," circulated widely after its publication in *From the Ashes* because of her direct indictment of American capitalism itself as the system responsible for Watts. McKellar begins the essay with a brief history of Watts, noting that it had always been an underdeveloped area where, after the expansion of the city following the labor boom of World War II, predatory merchants from outside the neighborhood established exploitative businesses. McKellar substantiates her claims with research on comparative pricing among stores inside and outside the neighborhood, where price differences can be up to four times higher in Watts for basic groceries. McKellar adds that Watts residents have little choice, "with the transportation system being so poor . . . people find themselves trapped to buy in their own backyard" (214). Being poor is expensive, and though McKellar's essay might not have brought news to any particular Watts resident, she offered a collective voice for the community's experiences, and she gave context for outsiders with which to understand residents' attacks on local businesses. As is frequently the case in twentieth century riots, according to Joshua Clover, looting local businesses is effectively an attack on the market, refusing and resetting the price of commodities.[33] Though McKellar does not go so far as to claim the point, she continues in this vein, noting that housing, too, is vastly overpriced. Tiny houses with broken pipes, rat and roach infestations, and poor sanitation services set Watts on the verge of an epidemic, and were one to break out, "the people would die surer than a field of grain after an invasion of locust" (215). Manning Marable famously called this "the underdevelopment of Black America," referring to the separation and stagnation of African American communities as so much surplus labor depressing wages for corporate profit.[34] These "sub-proletariat" communities are sacrificed for the benefit of economic growth based on reduced taxes and governmental spending on social services.[35] When I say that Schulberg became attuned to the materiality of Workshop writers' lives, I mean both the conditions in which they lived and writing as a means of enduring those conditions.

Returning to Povinelli's engagement with Watts, we can think of Jordan Downs and the house on Mettler Street as those sites where misery meets racialization, and racism requires no on-the-spot racists to do its work. In this regard, endurance, rather than resistance constitutes the daily life of overcoming this spatial sequestration. Endurance is the source and site for inhabiting one's body, not simply beyond race but as an agency amid the lived experience of race. Protest, alternative forms of democratic participation, and finally writing—as McKellar and others make clear—are modes of endurance that are self-aware in naming the conditions that bear on their bodies. Although Schulberg did not fully understand his own pivot, he ended up shifting his priorities—and his own embodied sweat equity—from the biopolitics of racial identity to identification with the material substance of race, or from writing as the representation of race to writing as the endurance of racialization.

Given this context, it is no wonder that Schulberg's efforts veered from writing to real estate, as he prioritized the establishment of a safe, stable home for writers and artists, and a dedicated space for readings and performance—Frederick Douglass House. The house staked him to Watts well beyond a token appearance. He was obliged to pay the rent and to fund repairs on the house, first of all. In 1967 Schulberg's accountant wrote him a stern letter, warning that his Workshop expenditures were exceeding his income, and he pressed him to drop the Workshop and "devote [his] time to income producing activities" instead.[36] This is just one of many documents suggesting how Schulberg's leadership of the Workshop was rerouted into a series of frustrating financial interactions and property negotiations. Between 1966 and 1967 he wrote dozens of letters to friends and acquaintances seeking funding support, and a daisy-chain of communications with the recently formed NEA, which was prepared to offer a grant to the Workshop, provided Schulberg could match it with new donations. However, the fundraising campaign yielded surprisingly little by way of contributions, and instead became a paper-generating machine, with Schulberg soliciting money and writing thank you notes for donations of twenty-five, fifty, or occasionally one hundred dollars. Few of Schulberg's supposedly deep-pocket Hollywood friends came through, and many including Frank Sinatra, Steve Allen, and Norman Mailer claimed to be cash strapped, suffering a bad year, or already tapped out for their annual contributions to charity.[37] Though he was often derided by local black nationalists as an elite, white outsider, Schulberg's archive during this period suggests he was harnessed to his project, obliged to extol, cajole, exhort, and testify on behalf of the Workshop.[38]

Meanwhile, the constant fundraising meant Schulberg had less time to read Workshop drafts and to provide leadership or vision. Schulberg's archives from this period include a folder of Workshop manuscripts from 1966 whose variety suggests the vitality of the Workshop, but also Schulberg's struggle to attend to his self-assigned task.[39] Fiction, prose essays, poetry; some of it typed, mimeographed, hand-written; held together with staples, corner-crimps, and sewing thread—the manuscripts testify to the variety of modes and means of writing, to the endurance of the writers, and to the sheer quantity of thought and perspective Watts residents wished to share. But the drafts demonstrate little evidence of actually being *read* by Schulberg. Margin notes appear on some of the poetry, though most of the fiction bears little or none. Indeed, one letter from a Workshop participant complains of Schulberg's lack of feedback, stating that this is not at all what he expected when he signed up. As a bisection of how Schulberg was spending his time in 1966, the folder gives the impression of a life transformed.[40]

Amid the daily paper chase, Schulberg's primary goal in 1966–1967 was to secure the building that would eventually become Frederick Douglass House. The house would include a workshop meeting room, living space for several Workshop participants, and a theater and performance facility. Schulberg and his brother scouted several derelict properties near the old railroad tracks, and discovered to their surprise that some of the worst property was exorbitantly expensive. They ended up leasing property from Sidney Lester, whom they were convinced was a slumlord getting the upper hand on them, and then they suffered months-long, expensive delays in construction.[41] While awaiting construction, the Workshop began meeting at Harry Dolan's house, and Schulberg was frustrated and angry when the Workshop executive board voted to pay Dolan for use of his house.[42] Unwittingly, Schulberg had entered into the sort of real estate arrangements that Workshop writers had described, both as a leaser and as property holder seeking maximum value for his investments. Initially, Schulberg believed in the efficacy of writing as representation, but his shift to developing a space for writing suggests a deeper comprehension of the conditions of deprivation in Watts, first of all, and how writing could be a form of endurance, a "mattering forth" (as Povinelli would put it) of protest against that deprivation. All the while, Schulberg's own material investments in Watts shifted his relationship to the project, from landlord to stakeholder, or, to provoke a bit, from a Beverly Hills writer to a Watts writer. I don't mean to say he became black, or even comparably dispossessed, as so many of his writers were, and he obviously had the freeway as his conduit back to his relatively luxurious home and otherwise worry-free lifestyle. What I do mean to say is that Schulberg became the neighbor to Watts, well beyond what he forecast or even imagined. By "neighbor" I mean that his proximity to Watts obviated his universalizing faith in liberation through representation, and afforded an *embodied* comprehension of Watts dispossession.

The command from Leviticus—to love the neighbor as your-self—invokes both borders and lines, approach and distance, a kind of spacing that reconstructs relations between self and other and sustains both difference and mutuality. Thought of as a kind of proximity, neighbor love need not be intentional, as in the case of Schulberg, nor does it bear some sort of preset political agenda. Rather, the obligation to love the other as yourself arrives in the borderland of ethics and politics, with "love" existing as an independent if problematic mode of relation, pertaining to neither domain. In "Peace and Proximity," Emmanuel Levinas insisted that an ethics of love for the other necessarily sustains otherness, prior to its eclipse in leveling notions of justice.[43] So, ethics precedes politics. Similarly, theorists of the ethics of the neighbor contend that we do not love the other because he is our neighbor, but create a neighborhood through our love—so, love precedes and perhaps constitutes the political. But what about material difference that manifests as racial differentiation—the otherness of the other? Writing on Augustine, Hannah Arendt observed that loving the other as yourself means loving as God does, but given that the self is worldly—that is, political—it also means sustaining the ineluctable differences that pertain in the material world.[44] There is no way of sorting the other into an ideal subject and a political subject, loving one and disregarding the other. Worse, we may construct a neighborhood out of love, but we also protect what we love, and it is not clear how to keep that protection from resolving into paranoia. Indeed, it is clear that we do not; paranoia reigns, gated communities proliferate, and social identities, like national identities, are policed and surveilled, as the example of George Zimmerman shooting Trayvon Martin makes clear. As

I make the transition to this next section, a conversation between
Schulberg and Baldwin, I invoke the neighbor to separate the two
dimensions of Schulberg's work, the love of the other, or the attempt
to overcome difference through writing, and the political reckoning with racialized oppression. Though I characterize this shift as a
movement toward a more effective engagement with the writers of
Watts, it seems clear that Schulberg himself did not understand his
project in those terms. Even as he shifted toward space-making, he
regarded it as so much frustration and distraction, and in the years
after the Workshop's demise, he always spoke more of the writing
than the place. I'll leave it at that—Schulberg was no social theorist, not even an intellectual, really, and with what follows I look to
Baldwin's critique of Schulberg's failure to understand—or perhaps
to effectively articulate—his relationship to race and racism.

EL DORADO

Schulberg spoke of racial identities as if they were metaphorical names
one inhabits but which are not, finally, identical with a person. For
Schulberg, it was the relative lightness of the metaphor, the easy substitutability of names, that made them both useful and disposable. Baldwin agreed about their disposability, but saw them as fundamentally
pernicious, especially when the *metonymical* dimensions of identity are
disregarded. For Baldwin racial names materialize through contingent
history and geography, and though Schulberg's work brought him into
proximity with Watts, Baldwin seems frustrated that his friend could
not recognize the real worth of this sort of neighboring.

Schulberg felt especially stung when he was rejected by black nationalists, including Dick Gregory, the prominent black entertainer
who in particular dismissed the Workshop, and he appealed to Baldwin
for support during a conversation that ranged across several months in
different locations, and which was redacted for publication in a 1966
article in *Playboy* magazine titled, "Dialog in Black and White."[45]

Across their conversation, the two writers daringly put all the topics and terms of racial conflict on the table, though they viewed these terms from dramatically different perspectives, and approached them with rather different stakes. Initially seeking a borderlands of common ground, the two found the dividing lines of difference instead. Like those who trade the phrases "black lives matter" and "all lives matter," Baldwin and Schulberg differently prioritized the politics and ethics of racial reconciliation, and the conversation reveals how the universalism of the latter phrase is impossible prior to the acknowledgment of the material particularity of the former.

The conversation between Schulberg and Baldwin as redacted for publication tilts toward Schulberg's defense of Jewish liberalism and the pursuit of civil rights remedies for racial injustice; however, the much longer version appearing in the unpublished transcripts and notes reveals an entirely different discussion, in which Baldwin is the one to repeatedly bring up Jewishness, with Schulberg querying black consciousness.[46] Schulberg begins by telling Baldwin that his understanding of black strife in Watts means "maybe I am able to 'think black,' too. It all depends on what we mean by 'thinking black.' Maybe I don't think as black as Malcom X, but I have a hunch I think a hell of a lot blacker than the Urban League or the brass of the NAACP."[47] Schulberg supports this startling claim by explaining, "'[T]hinking Black' sounds like an absolute, but it's a relative term—there are so many shades of black, so many shades of white" (281). Schulberg's claim is based on understanding, which is not the same as identification, nor is it exactly black consciousness. Rather, to "think black" is to be conscious of the specific experiences of deprivation black people suffer, and to understand how those experiences prompt radical reaction. Attempting to get on common footing with Schulberg, Baldwin begins his interrogation by asking him what exactly "Jewish" means to him, and Schulberg finally responds that Jesus Christ is his ideal Jew. There is a humorous moment in the transcription when Baldwin asks Schulberg to repeat himself—"[Y]our ideal Jew is what?"—as if he can't believe what he is hearing.[48] But Schulberg doubles down, assigning Jesus a role among the Hebrew prophets, paraphrasing from Matthew 25, "'if you do it to the least of mine, you do it to me'—that idea—an enormous idea—an idea of brotherhood, of empathy, that if lived up to, really *lived*, would solve our problem." It's a revealing moment for Schulberg, veering from an ethnic to an ethical Jewishness, away from parochialism and toward universalism, floating free from the American grammar of race. This sort of aphoristic, universal Jewishness ungrounded in any particular historical or geographical context perhaps helps explain the line about thinking black: both are metaphors of a moral point of view, and neither bears the complicated historical and geographical contingencies of racial identity.

Baldwin responds by adding textures of history and geography to Jewishness that Schulberg's universalism leaves out, effectively challenging one theory of social identity with another. Baldwin tells Schulberg, "I, as a Negro, and I think this may be true for most of the Negroes of my generation—well, I'm also a kind of Jew."[49] There is a subtle but important shift from Schulberg's "I can think black" to Baldwin's claim to be "a kind of Jew," for though both involve a figurative identity, Baldwin's "Jewish" (and identity in general for Baldwin) is more dynamic, more psychologically overdetermined, both more transposable *and* more enduring than Schulberg's. To put it another way, Schulberg's Jewish ethics sidesteps the politics of identification, while Baldwin aims to sustain the ethical *and* the political at work in Jewish identification. For Baldwin, identities are braided out of history, memory, and experience, and that braid puts the kink in otherwise optimistic accounts of ethical recognition.

Baldwin is quick to note the contingency of his claim for Jewishness, explaining that his identification is specific to his generation, raised in households where Hebraic narratives of exodus and return, along with prophetic stories of damnation and salvation, formed the consciousness of so many black men and women. Baldwin follows by crossing the universalizing metaphorical "Jew" with an account that is more contingently local, rerouting from ethics back to ethnicity:

I don't mean to say—I'm not making any claims on Jewish history. But I mean this—I mean that when I was in Jerusalem, *physically* in Jerusalem, I thought at once of my own immediate past and I thought of all my black forebears and how they used the word, "Jerusalem," and what it had meant to them. I didn't think of King David or Solomon, or any of that. I thought of my father—who was also, in a strange way, a creation of the Old Testament.[50]

The passage is remarkable for the way it restores the relation of metaphor to metonymy. Baldwin's father is the metaphorical Jew, "created" through his identification with the Hebrew bible, while Baldwin, by proxy, is the metonymical Jew. Of course, black American Hebraic identification in the 1920s and 1930s is itself a knot of ethics and politics—the metaphorical and the metonymical—and Baldwin begins to untangle those threads as he continues, "[N]ow, I was on my way to Africa the first time I found myself in Jerusalem. And I couldn't help wondering which homeland would have meant the most to my father. Which made me wonder, of course, which homeland meant the most to *me*. And this led to a whole Chinese box of wonderment."[51]

The claim to dual homelands mutually complicates each, for Africa is the more historically distant, Jerusalem the more proximate, the home of his father's memory. The African American identification with Jerusalem, of course, is contextualized by black Atlantic slavery, with "Jerusalem" as the imagined destiny of manumission. The black interpolation of Hebraic scripts inserts the brutal histories of capture and geographies of displacement into what had become for mid-twentieth-century American Jews an immaterial narrative of mythic return. In any case, identity for Baldwin involves both the history of displacement (Africa) and a metaphorical geography of return (Jerusalem), necessitating an ironical stance toward a nonetheless deeply felt pull of identification.

As the conversation continues, Schulberg attempts to regain ground, and repeatedly tells Baldwin that he believes identity has no real content, and should make no *political* difference, that it should neither give nor withhold special rights and privileges, but Baldwin turns the table and resignifies the political meaning of American Jewishness from the subjective view of black Americans:

Most American Jews have never seen—you know—Israel. The Promised Land. . . . They don't, after all, really need it—they don't intend to go there—they certainly don't need it as much as I need to know there's a place to go, in case I have to run. And I grew up paying Jews and being victimized by Jews—Jewish landlords and Jewish pawn-brokers—I don't know if the welfare workers were Jewish actually—but they all operated as kind of middle-men—or mid-wife—to our humiliation. So being in Jerusalem was a very funny kind of psychological collision for me.[52]

I've kept the whole quote to sustain the dramatic pivot from a general critique of Jewish diasporic consciousness to a loaded and personal critique of Jewish exploitation of black vulnerability. Insofar as Jewishness is metaphorically available to Baldwin, it signals a release from oppression, with geography functioning as nothing other than a pliable metaphor. But as sign of proximate, material experience, the contiguity of blacks and Jews is linked with harassment and exploitation, with Jews administering black property. Writing on Baldwin's political theory, George Shulman explains that Baldwin investigates the epistemic bases and affective denials that compose the realm of the political itself, so that he can say "black" and then reject that term, can claim "Jewishness" and then attack Jews, on the way to exposing how the myths of belonging and exclusion are the bases of our democratic norms.[53] For Baldwin, the universal or metaphorical Jew has to be squared with the proximate, American Jew, with "Jew" not a blanket identity (that is, Baldwin is not being anti-Semitic), but a contingently American social construct.

Baldwin is homing in on a thesis less about Jewishness and more about U.S. identification, as he goes on to say—much to Schulberg's consternation—that the African was in America before the Jew, arguing that immigrants to the United States trade in their immigrant identity for an ethnic whiteness. That swap is not assimilation but an interpolation into regimes of domination that afford privilege to white people and sustain the capacity of the United States to be an exceptional "land of immigrants" in the first place. He insists to Schulberg, "[T]he question for me isn't whether or not there's any hope for a Negro in a white-majority society; the question is whether or not the society is able to free itself of these obsolete terms and become, in effect, and joyously, color-blind," adding "All that jazz, *Negro, Jewish*—it's pure bullshit. These terms are used to hide from every one of us, including at this moment, you and me, the *real* disaster in this country—the failure of morality that is produced by a failure of identity."[54] No wonder Schulberg was confused, as he finds his friend initially parrying and redeploying "these obsolete terms," only to turn around and indict them. Identity categories are the "failure" because they are invented to perpetuate the "real disaster," economic exploitation that depends on, and thus continually invents and deploys, the material substance of race. Race is precisely the "failure" that hides in plain sight, and foregrounding it as Baldwin does, and as the organizers of Black Lives Matter do, is the starting point for reckoning with the moral failures of competitive capitalism. When *freedom* means secure property values and protection from the poor and the brown—in Baldwin's and Schulberg's moment, or our own—it is not enough to wish for full freedoms for all, regardless of identity, when identity itself is what secures "freedom." For Baldwin, obviating racial designations will not help Watts, but resignifying black anger as the justifiable response to white supremacy, and black nationalism as the confrontation of white nationalism, may be the starting point for a clear-sighted critique of structural inequality in the United States.

It is finally on the subject of property that Baldwin is able to clarify for Schulberg the scope of his critique of race, as both a locally

constructed phenomenon maintained through daily practices of deprivation and a broadly enduring social system of classification that
is naturalized by capitalism's optical illusion of equality. Baldwin's critique springs from the authors' discussion of the passage of Proposition
14, and he turns the critique directly at the material bases underlying
inequality, suggesting that identity is something more than language
or even consciousness. It is geography itself:

[referring to Los Angeles] Out there in the American El Dorado, that unmitigated horror of a place . . . ain't a damn thing paid for out there, they're
all living in terror of the poor-house—American back-bone! If your Cadil-
lac and your swimming pool aren't paid for and you know you can't go any
further West—the next stop is Tokyo, God help us, which is east—then, of
course, any black boy or Mexican coming anywhere *near* your monstrously
mortgaged joint—which is *all you have*—is an intolerable threat. And it's
on this level the country lives, *that's* our society. Then, when the riots come,
they tremble for their unpaid-for swimming pool and ask "what does the
Negro want?" And all *that* bull-shit, and ask the Negro to respect the law.
What law? The law which has just robbed him of any possibility of moving
out of the ghetto and beats him and brutalizes him—in order to protect
their swimming pools?[55]

Baldwin's diagnosis of the Watts riot associates the campaigners for
Prop 14 with the generally affluent of California, all under the sign
of "El Dorado"—the wager for profit underwriting colonial expansion and extermination. In this case, El Dorado is retroactively created through the production of scarcity and exclusivity that requires
an enemy outsider. The worse Watts is—and Compton, Inglewood,
and East L.A.—the more valuable the real estate on the Westside of
L.A. In Southern California, where so much wealth exists as rising
home equity—"which is *all you have*"—nothing would plunge real
estate prices faster than dissipating fear of black and brown people,
integrating housing and schools, combined with the growth in real
estate value distributed more evenly across Los Angeles.

So we arrive at the crux of the argument between Schulberg and Baldwin, and the quandary of any attempt to think of the ethics of the neighbor through the politics of property, or material inequality more generally: the neighbor's ethical responsibility for the other depends upon that otherness (especially in Levinas), yet it also aims to erase it (in common terms, to move "beyond race"). This is an ethics of the neighbor without actual neighborhoods. It is one thing to say that ethics precedes politics, as Levinas does at times. It is quite another to suggest that ethics can somehow erase the political bases of recognizability, and it may even be the case that the field wherein the ethical encounter may be possible is itself only made possible by a politics of inequality. For Baldwin, love of the neighbor doesn't ignore, obviate, or precede identity. Rather, love is what exposes identity's failure, as Baldwin explains in *The Fire Next Time:* "[L]ove takes off the masks that we fear we cannot live without and know we cannot live within," explaining, "I use the word 'love' here not merely in the personal sense but as a state of being, or a state of grace—not in the infantile American sense of being happy but in the tough and universal sense of quest and daring and growth."[56]

Baldwin's critique of Schulberg demonstrated how his ethical responsibility to Watts depended on the prior distinction of Watts and Beverly Hills, which Schulberg recognized, but could not imagine eliminating. For Baldwin, responsibility for the other would require a radical elimination of the conditions of otherness. El Dorado is always an atavistic myth of the future that requires a past and a place from which you are escaping—and until you can understand that you are living squarely within that myth, there is no hope in proffering your version of a prosperous future for anyone else. Baldwin was trying to explain to Schulberg that racial ontology is not or not simply a form of consciousness, nor is it a language. Rather, race materializes through the instruments of law; through the strategic use of capital; through municipal elections, backroom development deals, and freeway construction. Crossing borders, Schulberg missed the lines and specifically misunderstood how the lines of division were drawn and sustained in the first place. Getting "beyond race" can only be accomplished by getting further into race, or by understanding how racial assignment works in the first place.

The Workshop earned two NEA grants and pioneered a replicable model for subsequent workshop development around California, and then across the country. Schulberg moved to New York, where he expanded the Workshop model to Harlem and the Bronx. Meanwhile, in Watts Frederick Douglass House thrived too well, and manager Harry Dolan was often in a bind, navigating the competing demands of Panthers, cultural nationalists, and writers who simply wanted to write. With the arrival of Panther activists in the Workshop, the FBI— already actively sabotaging groups across Watts—installed a plant, Darthard Perry, code-named "Othello," who sabotaged the Workshop's facilities, fomented political friction, and eventually burned down Douglass House. Though Watts was briefly the object of national attention, and the subject of documentaries, congressional inquiries, and journalistic investigations, by 1972 the complex political and arts scenes of Watts were swapped out of the national imagination for Norman Lear's ludic vision in *Sanford and Son*, a sitcom about a Watts junk dealer and his unemployed son (meanwhile, the inspirational banner phrase of black power, "move on up," was dragooned into the theme song for Lear's sitcom *The Jeffersons*, about a conservative black businessman whose family "moves on up" to an upper-East-Side apartment in New York City).

But before it was burned down, Frederick Douglass House was briefly a metaphor of an improbable cohabitation of disparate people with diverging politics, housed under the same symbolic roof, neighbors to each other, cooperating who knows how—that is, a metaphor of a metonymy. Writing for the 1970 issue of the *Negro American Literature Forum* (the precursor to *African American Review*) Workshop writer Talmadge Spratt poetically described Frederick Douglass House as a gathering of black poets, musicians, and orators, including

"Malcom X . . . and Medgar Evers and Martin Luther King, Jr., too, issuing edicts to the world that all black men have the right to have dreams."[57] Malcolm, Medgar, Martin—a triad of black men whose legacies were as yet unsettled in Los Angeles, and who could be viewed as offering concretely different models for emancipation.

Last but far from least, [Douglass House] is Budd Schulberg, the ofay, blue-eyes white devil who put his own successes on the chopping block to ferret out pen men and women who could record deeds and/or aggrandizements that lay dormant and disregarded in a supposedly free and democratic Western World. Douglass House exists. For real. It is our thing. And it's about time.[58]

I don't think Schulberg himself ever claimed the meaning of the metaphor, that he, along with Malcom, Martin, and Medgar, constituted the house—or, he only understood the metaphor, and not the metonymy, that is, the implications of being contiguous with those men. If Schulberg didn't claim the broader implications—if he was never able to translate the brief success of the Workshop into a politics of liberation—Baldwin's critique of Schulberg might get us there.

UNMITIGATED BLACKNESS

I close this chapter with an examination of Paul Beatty's 2015 novel *The Sellout*, set in Compton, a city bordering on Watts in greater Los Angeles County and a site of the 1992 riots following the acquittal of police officers charged with assaulting Rodney King.[59] The novel is set in the South Central L.A. neighborhood of "Dickens," modeled after the true-life neighborhood of Richland Farms, set in the eastern edge of Compton. Like the fictional Dickens, Richland Farms is a vestigial agricultural zone in the heart of urban L.A. County, with large lots adjacent to the Compton creek, which dribbles into the Los Angeles River (in fact, little more than a concrete-bed stream), where residents raise livestock and grow crops.[60] Richland Farms was permanently designated an agricultural zone in 1888, when Reverend Griffith Dickenson Compton incorporated the land that would become the city of Compton. Generations of residents of Compton can recall visiting the animals, or simply seeing riders on horseback moseying up the street, and for as strange as that seems, it's worth recalling that South Central Los Angeles, including Watts, was once heavily agricultural. Indeed, as the celebrated independent film *Killer of Sheep* observes, Watts was home to a stockyard and slaughterhouse in the 1960s, and many of South Central L.A.'s black residents descend from families that migrated from the Southern agricultural belt in the 1930s though 1950s. Beatty's novel is about the erasure of the historical and geographical past, and the return of formal segregation marks out how those erasures occlude ongoing, systemic, environmental racism. The novel's characters and especially the narrator suffer from what psychologist Glenn Albrecht calls "solostalgia," an existential distress that occurs when drastic environmental change disconnects you from the place in which you live.[61] In Beatty's novel, though everyone remains right where they have always been, Dickens disappears from the map, and the city's distribution of social value changes around them, further isolating them from the material growth and property value increase characteristic of Los Angeles.

The Sellout reads like a narrative coda to the Schulberg-Baldwin conversation, demonstrating both the invented or metaphorical condition of racial assignment and the spatial materialization of race. At the same time, Beatty ventures a version of love of the neighbor that neither universalizes nor essentializes its subject; blackness is neither obviated, nor reified, and the novel sits on the seam between a pessimistic account of blackness as that which is produced as the negative other of capitalist structures and an optimistic account of the ownership of the space of negation as the place of refusal. Fred Moten provides a poetic description of the spacing of pessimism and optimism that resonates with the spatial terms used in this book thus far: "Black optimism and Afro-pessimism are asymptotic. Which one is the curve and which one is the line? It doesn't matter."[62] Moten's term, *asymptotic*, is a mathematical concept of a line and a curve that approach each other but never meet; lacking intersection, they nonetheless remain mutual to each other, and the in-between is the space both of negation and of possibility. As with so many black-studies scholars, Moten's critical agenda is historical, but he continually figures history in spatial terms, with the curve and the line suggesting the production of race as the production of space. Residing in the gap, for Moten, is love, which is not an evasion of either history or geography but an engagement with blackness that evades the ontological traps set by Western philosophy's dependence on and production of a negative racial substance.

Moten's curve and line recall other delineations of space in this book, most prominently the freeway that Schulberg would drive from Beverly Hills to Watts, an optimistic transect from Schulberg's point of view, though when driving the same route Baldwin would conclude pessimistically that Beverly Hills and Watts could never connect. Different from Moten's curve and line, between Schulberg and Baldwin the very same freeway functions entirely differently, as a site of access and joining—the fluid space of a border to be crossed—and as the demarcation of a boundary—a line of eternal separation. The critical question in common here is whether blackness is something that can positively engage whiteness, through workshops and publications say, or whether blackness is ontologically produced as the effect of whiteness and can therefore only stake its claim by attacking the philosophical tradition that produces racial ontology in the first place. Baldwin did not go that far, did not seem to believe in racial ontology in the first place, and typically deployed a more labile psychological language to talk about white desire, love, and its negations. For Baldwin, love could link incommensurable spaces, which was enough to allow his interlocution with Schulberg. Moten's never-joining curve and line give us something more complex, the "para-ontological" space between an optimistic account of the possibilities of black critique and a pessimistic account of the being of blackness as nothing other than a negation constructed by whiteness. Though Moten does not write about space per se, his recurring use of spatial metaphors (I will cite more further on) to describe the place of black critique suggests, once again, that we follow Lefebvre's hint, that we step off the metaphorical tightrope hung in the air above material space and ground ourselves instead in the materiality of racial assignment.

In Chapter 1, we saw that this grounding effectively organized the plot of *Their Dogs Came with Them*, with Tranquilina initially rejecting her inheritance of the gift of flight and choosing instead to remain among the earthly subjects of her missionary love. Flight connoted possibility in that novel, but the possible was yoked to the believable, with belief itself organized by and through material conditions: you believe what you make possible in the world. We can believe Tranquilina believes because we witness her selfless care of the most vulnerable people of East L.A. Similarly and even more grounded is the work of *Union de Vecinos*, which materializes the metaphors of the Christian bible, in line with the philosophy of Liberation Theology. Doing so, UV creates spaces for material miracles, where the miraculous is the effect of the reconstruction of a neighborhood of possibility. In less religious terms, this practice amounts to "negotiating space," or transforming lines of division into borders of encounter. Corners, courtyards, alleyways, and intersections that had been the provenance of drug dealers, gang members, and police have become reinscribed as neighborhoods. Negotiation is not elimination, and the neighborhood remains an open set.

What Viramontes describes and what UV practices is a reclamation of a neighborhood within a centuries-long struggle for spaces of identification by people of Mexican descent in the Americas. Notably, neither the novel nor the neighborhood organization put social identity at the center of their respective projects. There are Chicana/os in *Their Dogs Came with Them*, and East L.A. has been one of the centers of Chicana/o social activism since the early 1970s, but neither the novel nor the community project are existentially about identity. The political practices of redlining and urban development that isolate and immiserate East L.A. are themselves identity projects, depressing and policing the lives of those whose racial origins have been officially defined as degenerate. In contrast, the contested project at the heart of Schulberg and Baldwin's conversation is whether or not identity can be the basis of social critique, and if so, how.

Beatty takes up the same question and a similar motif of lines that both mark out the reality of racial segregation and delineate a space of belonging and possibility. There is the chalk line around the dead body of the narrator's father, who is shot while contesting a driving ticket. The narrator's father was a well-known academic psychologist, who researched the effects of environmental racism (typically using his son as his research subject), and his murder, for which no officer is held accountable, marks the isolation and vulnerability that comes with geographical invisibility. Then there are the borderlines of the neighborhood itself, which have suddenly disappeared from municipal maps, along with freeway signs and even news channel weather forecasts that would publicly confirm the neighborhood's distinct existence. The novel's plot begins at this point, as the narrator takes on the project of restoring Dickens to the map, first with his own inked-in circumscription on the iconic Los Angeles Thomas Guide map. From there, more lines follow: freeway signs of the narrator's crafting that point the way to Dickens, bus routes that routinely take lines of flight from the proscribed route to service the narrator's restoration project, and finally a physical border the narrator paints on the street around the entire neighborhood. Like a scene out of a Viramontes story, only spun for comedy, elderly Dickens residents see the paint job and intuitively understand its purpose, falling into reveries for when the neighborhood had both identity and community. Still, the comedy here and elsewhere is underwritten by melancholy, as the narrator reflects on the borderline and notes how "the jagged way it surrounded the remnants of the city reminded me of the chalk outline the police had needlessly drawn around my father's body" (109).

Here again we have a "curve and line," a geographical zone and a narrative space where optimism and possibility run proximate to melancholy and constraint. However, in *The Sellout*, the narrator's optimism always remains cynical, operating within the sort of zero-sum logic of human and property value that Baldwin outlined for Schulberg as the racial constitution of Los Angeles, and the United States in general. The narrator concludes that the disappearance of Dickens in the first place was "part of a blatant conspiracy by the surrounding, increasingly affluent . . . communities to keep their property values up," with neighboring communities renamed as "Crest View, La Cienega Heights, or Westdale[,] even though there weren't any topographical features like crests, views, or heights to be found within ten miles" (58). Sentences like these, so very funny and perfectly accurate, may be what Beatty is referring to when he rebuffs the label of "satirist," for here the comedy lies not in the author's invention but in the absurd reality he properly documents.[63] The narrator offers an analysis that riffs on Mike Davis's Marxian history of Los Angeles in *City of Quartz*: "Nowadays Angelenos who used to see themselves as denizens of the west, east, and south sides wage protracted legal battles over whether their two-bedroom charming country cottages reside within the confines of Beverlywood or Beverlywood Adjacent" (58).[64] The atomization of Los Angeles is prompted by the migration of minorities out of traditionally segregated neighborhoods—"Too Many Mexicans," as one chapter title puts it—so rebranding small communities becomes a way of shoring up status through racial exclusion of ethnic others.

Among the effects of this sort of cynical cartography is the production of melancholic spaces, which the narrator calls "racism vortexes":

Spots where visitors experience deep feelings of melancholy and ethnic worthlessness. Places like the breakdown lane on the Foothill Freeway, where Rodney King's life, and in a sense America and its haughty notions of fair play, began their downward spirals. Racial vortices like the intersection of Florence and Normandie, where misbegotten trucker Reginald Denny caught a cinder block, a forty-ounce, and fucking centuries of frustration in the face. (129)

The long quote exemplifies Beatty's linkage of disparate social phenomena: racial violence, personal violence, and a deep melancholy of place are all connected. Drawing a through-line to show the consequential connections across history and geography exposes "the normative organizational codes that cohere in oppressive power systems," as Judith Madera has described it. *The Sellout* may be what Madera characterizes as a literature of "black flow," which "find[s] disruptions in, contradictions to, and corridors through these codes."[65] In *The Sellout*, the chalk line around the narrator's dead father does not function as site of investigation—there will be no inquiry into the father's killing—but as image to be decoded and redeployed by the narrator. The chalk line says, "This is how we wield our power," and the narrator's appropriation of the line for his cartography may indeed function as a "corridor" through the codes of racism. Drawing the boundary line around Dickens, then, is a way of making visible the common vulnerability of the neighborhood's residents, first of all, and a way of inscribing identity as the geographical experience of that vulnerability. Blackness is manifest as the dead zone within the chalk line, the invisible neighborhood within the borderline, and the ostensible segregation matters forth a black identity able to claim itself in solidarity and opposition to racist policing.

The distinction between the chalk line and the borderline can be hard to see: Does returning Dickens to the map really matter? The novel holds open a space of distinction simply through its wicked comedy, as Beatty doubles down on a logic of pride and racial uplift, taking it to a perverse extreme. Hominy, the last surviving member of the "The Little Rascals" and the narrator's neighbor, foists himself upon the narrator at the start of the novel, declaring himself the narrator's slave and insisting that only through repeated abuse and humiliation can he feel free. Hominy contributes scant labor to the narrator's farm, and the narrator satisfies Hominy's desire for humiliation by paying for a high-priced dominatrix (one of several instances in which *The Sellout* borrows from the prop-box of Melville's *Benito Cereno*). It is Hominy who goes on to compare his regime of humiliation with the narrator's cartography scheme, declaring, "the whip feels good on the back, but the sign feels good in the heart," suggesting that Hominy's degradation and the narrator's pride are co-constituted by a common logic of racial materialism, in which the renewal of a marginal black neighborhood simply reiterates the logic that co-constitutes whiteness and property.[66] The redrawing of Dickens's borderline comforts Hominy, as it helps fans seeking autographs and plantation-style stories actually find him, and the narrator effectively redraws the color line in another bid to please his "slave." He begins by installing a "whites only" sign on the local bus, driven by his sometimes girlfriend, Marpessa, and he hires a white actor to kick Hominy out of his seat, sending him to the back—a move Hominy finds wholly satisfying. The sign remains on the bus for weeks, bringing a kind of satisfaction to locals who feel that it at least provides a script for what is otherwise the unacknowledged reality of racial segregation.

Later, when his school principal friend tells him about her undermotivated students, the narrator mocks up a billboard at a nearby construction site announcing the building of a new, very elite, whites-only school, and sure enough, the plan works. Here is how the narrator puts it:

Even in these times of racial equality, when someone whiter than us, richer than us, blacker than us, Chineser than us, better than us, whatever than us, comes around throwing their equality in our faces, it brings out our need to impress, to behave, to tuck in our shirts, do our homework, show up on time, make our free throws, teach, and prove our self-worth in hopes that we won't be fired, arrested, or trucked away and shot. (208)

As with prior quotations, I've kept the entire sentence to demon-strate how Beatty's writing draws together a series of perceptions, at once humorous and seemingly satirical, but finally sharply insight-ful and brutally realistic. We notice, for instance, the way *equality* appears twice in the sentence, first as the putative state of modern, color-blind life and then as a tool of racial domination and social erasure along the lines of "all lives matter." Similarly subversive is the equivocation of tucking in our shirt and making our free throws, suggesting that black achievement is finally only thinkable as athletic achievement. Finally, the payoff of segregation—though couched in the Booker T. Washington language of social uplift—is nothing other than the hoped-for avoidance of what can only read as the headlines of the week, where black men, women, and children are killed by police with startling, agonizing frequency. This is why Be-atty resists the "satire" label. No "modest proposal," his character's plan to segregate Dickens simply underscores the present reality that the neighborhood and its schools are already segregated. Likewise, though this and other passages skewer the false memory that black people were better off during segregation, it confronts the possibil-ity that contemporary black vulnerability is on par with the mid-twentieth century, pre-civil-rights period.

Beatty's ironical turn on "equality" recalls Baldwin's similar rebuff of a discourse of "equality" in *The Fire Next Time*: "People are not . . . terribly anxious to be equal (equal, after all, to what and to whom?) but they love the idea of being superior."[67] Superiority is differential, requiring and proliferating boundaries, while equality is a fiction of equal access, a border-free life. And as Beatty makes clear, the boundaries exist already, whether one wishes to acknowledge them or not. L.A.'s freeway system creates the boundaries of black and brown neighborhoods such as Compton in South Central L.A. and Boyle Heights in East L.A., which are literally surrounded and walled off by freeways in all directions. These are the lines that distin-guish Watts from Beverly Hills, as Baldwin explained to Schulberg,

and they mark off the material conditions of neighbor relations that
would precede and determine any form of recognition. Borrowing
once again from Fred Moten,

> Within this framework blackness and antiblackness remain in brutally anti-
> social structural support of one another like the stanchions of an absent
> bridge of lost desire over which flows the commerce and under which flows
> the current, the logistics and energy of exclusion and incorporation, that
> characterizes the political world.[68]

The absent bridge tracing ever-ephemeral line bears all the weight
of California's property-based racial paranoia, manifesting variously
as freeway walls, gang tags, police districts, and even neighborhood
boundaries. In Beatty's novel, politics indeed simultaneously incorpo-
rates and excludes, and perpetuates, the differential logic of insiders
and outsiders, winners and losers that Baldwin lamented across his
career, and which Schulberg thought could be dispatched through
representation, right up until he became caught between these two
stanchions himself.

   This may be why, at the end of the novel, even as Beatty's narrator
is enjoying the success of his several-tiered segregation project—with
increased student performance and decreased crime—he laments that
this success requires blackness to be contingently tied to vulnerability,
loss, displacement, and above all whiteness. Instead, the narrator wishes
for what he calls "Unmitigated Blackness," which is defined neither in
terms of racial uplift nor pessimistic precarity, but as "the realization that
there are no absolutes," the acceptance that "nihilism makes life worth
living," and "simply not giving a fuck." This is a blackness that is not
controlled by time or space, not defined in dialectical relation with a
racial other, or pegged to an autonomous nationalist identity. Unmitigated Blackness is the narrator "sitting . . . on the steps of the Supreme
Court smoking weed, under the 'Equal Justice Under Law' motto," a
refusal of the controlling terms of racial recognition and of the fictions
of equality that occlude racialization.

No other form of recognition is saluted by the novel, and indeed it closes with the narrator's foil, Foy Cheshire, the neighborhood's resident black intellectual, celebrating the election of the nation's first black president, waving the American flag because, he says, "the United States of America has finally paid off its debts," another form of recognition that the narrator refuses, responding, "and what about the Native Americans? What about the Chinese, the Japanese, the Mexicans, the poor, the forests, the water, the air, the fucking California condor? When do they collect?" (289). The narrator's rejection of Chesire's celebration refuses the cash value of recognition and insists on redistributing the temporalized redemption as a list of categories of the trampled and exploited. Foy's term *debt* is unmistakably historicist, indicating payment for past crimes, and so overlooks the way race is sustained through geography, including the organization of material space and the distribution of rights of property. In this way, Beatty's novel engages and even upends the prioritization of history over geography that underwrites the Schulberg-Baldwin conversation and appears as the recurring spatial symbology of Moten's consideration of black ontology. Moten in his way is also querying the possibility of an "Unmitigated Blackness," though Beatty's list of American debts suggests that racism is sustained through a list of contingent practices that seemingly have nothing to do with race. The list itself is a metonymy, that is a spatial linkage, which puts the narrator's quest for "Unmitigated Blackness" in contingent relation with the material welfare of other racialized groups, and even the ecology of California itself. It is finally the space of Southern California that constitutes the narrator's project of recuperation, and until that ground is redistributed beyond the value-producing logic of exclusion, recognition matters not at all.

CHAPTER 3

MY NEIGHBORHOOD
Private Claims, Public Space,
and Jewish Los Angeles

"The quasi-logical presupposition of an identity between mental
space (the space of the philosophers and epistemologists) and
real space creates an abyss between the mental sphere on one
side and the physical and social spheres on the other. From time
to time some intrepid funambulist will set off to cross the void,
giving a great show and sending a delightful shudder through the
onlookers. By and large, however, so-called philosophical thinking
recoils at the mere suggestion of any such *salto mortale*. If they still
see the abyss at all, the professional philosophers avert their gaze."

Henry Lefebvre, *The Production of Space*[1]

HENRI LEFEBVRE's cheeky critique of philosophers of
space suggests the challenge of this chapter, and the rationale for placing it last rather than first among three. At the beginning of his path-
breaking Marxist analysis of space, *The Production of Space*, Lefebvre
observes that it's not so much the case that theorists have not previously discussed space, but that such discussions occur on high, looking
down from theory, naturalizing their own assumptions as objective understanding. The funambulist, or tightrope walker, is the one who attempts to bridge the connection between a theory of space as conceived
according to philosophical concepts and actual material space as it is
produced through various social forces. The *salto mortale* would be the
fall into material reality, which, for Lefebvre's cowardly philosophers,

would mean the death of preconceived theory. Rather than ignore, or perhaps worse, naturalize space, the philosopher should examine the *production* of space. In this book I have examined in my own way particular instances when space is produced through material, psychological, and ethical boundary formation and border crossing. Space is a matter of spacing—the organization of proximate relations among people—while spacing itself is determined by material conditions. At the same time, I have pluralized space, demonstrating how a given space affords access and entry for some, restriction and containment for others. Political subjectivity is not independent of space, but it is in fluid relation with it, shifting and changing as do spaces, as Viramontes demonstrates in *Their Dogs Came with Them*: Turtle moves as if in a cone of malevolence, yet her proximity to other characters seems to produce a penumbra of benevolence. These encounters, or moments of letting be, are not exactly ethical choices willed by any given character but the result of the arrangement of space that precedes and produces the encounters themselves. We necessarily cohabitate with others, and the spaces we build or wherein we dwell often determine the conditions of that cohabitation. Most of us have been proximate to others whose living conditions are vastly different from ours, as we pass through their neighborhoods by railway or freeway, rooftops and yard fencing nearly arms-reach close, while recognizing that the erstwhile proximity to the other is arranged and controlled by a political economy that precedes and guides, and so precludes, an ethics of encounter.

Before embarking on this chapter's theoretical investigation of the ethics of the neighbor, recall that the prior chapters examined material space in its economic, political, and affective dimensions, while analyzing the recombinations and reconstitutions of neighborhood spaces through their many uses. Any given space can give rise to multiple psychological states—anxiety, desire, joy, despair—depending on one's proximity to others, while the conditions of that proximity are determined by biopolitically governed spatial arrangements that often operate

beyond immediate or local view and perception. It is only upon analyzing these material dimensions of political space that we take Lefebvre's
dare to climb the ladder to the metaphorical tightrope and attempt to
perilously balance a theory of space with a material analysis of space. In
the previous chapters I have explored either the near miss of ethics or
the successful leap over the wall of political separation, and have prioritized material space as it is produced and experienced "on the ground."
In this third chapter I bring forward a topic that has been been in the
background but present all along, namely the figure of the neighbor as a
construct of ethics and politics. The neighbor, of course, populates Viramontes's and Beatty's fiction, and is the object of both UV and the Watts
Writers Workshop. In each instance, real places and people proximate
to each other are both subjects and objects of space-making endeavors,
from the construction of freeways to the construction of workshops,
from gang tags inscribing barriers to UV's tags inscribing community.
It is clear that the neighbor matters, but it is less clear how and why,
and in this chapter, about Jewish space in West Los Angeles, I will demonstrate how the neighbor is the crossroads of ethics and politics. I do
not advocate for "the neighbor" as a holy grail of politcal theory—the
source and answer to all manner of interracial connunudrums. Rather,
given the prior chapters' orbiting around neighbor matters, I conclude
with an extended exploration of how and why the neighbor recurs and
what this has to tell us about how we live with difference in a given
space. Here, then, I explore the theory and the practice of the neighbor.
"Practice," because that is what is all too often missing from theories of
the neighbor, which rarely engage with actual neighborhoods and actual
people, as mentioned in the Introduction. In other words, this chapter
is descriptive, rather than proscriptive. Even though the topic of ethics
is implicitly normative—ethics tell us what we "ought" to do—in this
chapter I more realistically explore how that sense of "ought" resolves
into and out of political formations, how it bears different weight in
different contexts, and how it finally exists as a through-line connecting
several projects across L.A.'s neighborhoods.

THE NEIGHBOR

A neighbor is someone both like and unlike me, less than kin but more than kind. The neighbor is someone to whom I am obligated but against whom I also defend myself and my family. The neighbhor is my political other, someone with whom I am competing for status and power; someone who agitates me because of the narcissism of small differences, as Freud would put it.[2] And most strange of all, the neighbor is also my substitution: I am my neighbor's neighbor, and the complex, competitive, and political stance I have toward him, he has toward me. I have neighbors with whom I have almost nothing in common—neither religious nor political positions, neither cultural tastes nor happy hobbies—but toward whom I feel a strong degree of care. If asked why, I'd surely admit that much of it comes down to property values: so long as my neighbors are well employed, take care of their homes, and work with me and others to keep up the neighborhood, we are allied. Can caring about someone for what are fundamentally political reasons also be ethical? The nearness of the neighbor (which is just what *neighbor* means— "the near one") introduces an intimacy to neighbor relations that I may not share with even my good friends, extending the question. Who else but the neighbor sees me in my pajamas when I get the morning paper, sees just how indolent I can be about lawn care, or knows to the minute the regularity of my weekly cycling schedule? All that intimacy, of course, can be discomfitting, and intimacy's cousin may be hostility. The moment I find my neighbor judging me, or perhaps the moment I judge my neighbor, it may all be over; I may find the neighbor's practices and habits intolerable (or he me) well beyond what I would tolerate in friends and family. If my neighbor and I team up to stop a newcomer from playing his music too loudly at night, we're tight. If my neighbor starts playing the music too loudly, he's going down.

Either the neighbor, then, is a salutory figure for the intersection of politics and ethics—a productive crossroads of theory—or the neighbor is fundamentally a partner in exclusion: the neighbor as figure of conspiracy and paranoia, the one with whom I collaborate against the other. In either case, this reflection is motivated by the deeply ambiguous yet centrally compelling commandment of Leviticus, "love thy neighbor as thyself," an injunction in which nearly every term challenges easy definition, and which would be dismissed in our age of irony but for the fact that it persists as a legacy of Western religious and political thought. Perhaps it is precisely the ambiguity of the command that allows all who comment on it to find in it what they wish. Never mind the vagaries of the neighbor—what is "love"? Why, Freud asked, should I spend out my precious love, which is a limited energy, after all, on someone other than my family? How do we understand the "self," espcially after Nietzche and Derrida, who teach us to be suspicious of any construct that presumes a clear relation between self and other, where "self" is always already anxiously harboring the other? And most vexing of all is the innocent-seeming prepositional cipher, "as"—as if we have any grasp on how we do or ought to love ourselves that we could draw from as a model for loving outward to the world around.

Neighbor relations are locally formed. The university where I teach was until recently open, and residents in the community could walk through campus on the way to a network of greenways and a shopping district beyond the campus. However, in response to drug-related crime, the university has installed a fence with a locking gate, making the pass-through imposing if not impossible for non-university residents of the neighborhood. The rationale for the fence is obvious—it secures a liability, I have been told—but its political and psychological effects are more complicated, and in any case, it does not seem to have stopped crimes involving students. I live right across the street from campus, and suffice it to say that I have seen the students at their worst, and am aware that when I reiterate that phrase "drug-related crime" I am simply masking the fact that the university students are buying and in some cases selling illegal drugs, on and off campus, in

my neighborhood; crime has not entered the neighborhood from outside, but is part of the neighborhood's composition, and a symptom of
the economy that exists between the campus community—in which
I include well-paid faculty and largely well-to-do students—and the
neighborhood just north of campus. Indeed, the university is separated
from its proximate territory by a six-lane thoroughfare named "University Boulevard," built under conditions and for reasons similar to
those discussed in the previous chapters, as a means of segregating this
small, southern city. My university administrators have begun to seek
ways to engage the neighborhood, seemingly as an ameliorative effort,
but as is often the case with these sorts of things, the engagement is
necssarily political, with one constituency far more empowered than
the other. Politics is the distribution of power and cannot yield justice if not predicated on and faithful to an ethics of reciprocity. Any
effort at changing the neighborhood without changing the campus
itself seems doomed to replicate and not alleviate the assymetries of
power and the politics of containment.

It would not take too much paraphrasing to read Levinas's essay
"Peace and Proximity," ostensibly about European policies toward
decolonized nations and their expatriate refugees residing in Europe,
as pertaining equally to both broad questions of human rights and
local questions of the neighborhood. After all, if the social absorption
of the foreign other is to be effectively accomplished, Europeans—or
Americans, or any nation, or any boundaried group of people heretofore believing themselves to be more alike than not—will have to
deal with the disturbing *difference* of the other. Levinas provocatively
enjoins his readers "to ask oneself if peace, instead of being the result of
an absorption or disappearance of alterity, would not on the contrary
be a *fraternal* mode of a proximity to the other," and he subsequently
insists that "proximity of the neighbor" is "the susception of dying for
the other. Peace with the other (*autrui*) goes that far. It is the whole
gravity of love of the neighbor, of love without concupiscence."[3] For
Levinas, a politics of justice that originates in notions of rationality

and universality ultimately invests the State with the power to wage
a war of all against all, or as Jacques Rancière has argued, deigns wars
of intervention as the necessary end of a concept of human rights.[4]
War presumes the consolidation of the nation under a single unified
banner, and while the enemy of the nation is likewise totalized, the
presumptive peace that war seeks likewise imagines a totalizing sameness. When we win, our enemy will submit and become more like us.
Even if you do not find that presumption ethically difficult to swal-
low, Western military adventures in the twenty-first century should
make it clear that this is just not how wars work. Only a politics that
begins in the ethics of the neighbor—that does not seek to absorb the
difference of the other, but takes responsibility for it—can structure a
justice predicated on love.

Levinas's "neighbor" depends on a spacing that is proximate and
open, and which does not resolve into something so simple as an alliance—joining together for advantange over others, other neighborhoods—or, when it does become an alliance, it signals the collapse of
ethics and the failure to remain faithful to the radical two-ness that
proximate spacing engenders. In his aggressive critique of Levinas's
ethics, Slavoj Žižek histrionically advocates "smashing the neighbor's
face," or what he perceives to be the seductive lie of ethics, but the violence of his metaphor suggests exactly what he misunderstands about
Levinas: Levinas's ethics, as Thomas Claviez argues, are metonymic;
the face is neither a literal face nor a metaphor for some version of the
human, but the alertness to the other's humanness that originates in
proximity.[5] Contrary to Žižek's reductive misreading, Levinas's neighbor implies no conspiracy because there is no collapse of otherness
into the same: neighbors, for Levinas, remain neighbors precisely because of unassimilable difference. Levinas's neighbor is never part of a
"we," and the ethics pertaining to his neighbor always open outward
into the strangeness of the other. Put another way, Levinas sustains
"nearness," which implies an approach as well as a gap—simultaneity
without sameness, or a striated geography over a smooth, flat map, to

118 CHAPTER 3

borrow from Deleuze and Guattari—where people experience place in different ways according to a broader field of social location.⁶ Levinas thus forcasts a cartography of ethics, one that maps responsibility by extending the boundaries of proximity while always maintaining proximity's preservation of alterity. Still, the contemporary usage of the word *neighbor* directs us toward both Levinas's ethics and Žižek's critique; the gated campus of my example shares the logic of both the gated community and the gated continent: an overtly hostile lockdown, outlining same and other.

Between world and community, I now pivot toward the city and transpose the ethical dimensions of the neighbor onto the ethnic coordinates of the city. Doing so risks the "salto mortale" Lefebvre describes, walking the line bteween a philosophy of the neighbor and the spatial arrangement of actual neighborhoods, including those often in conflict. Does Levinas's construct of spacing map onto the felt experience of space in a multiethnic city? Does the metonymic spacing of ethical difference metaphorize the politics of same and other undergirding the flux and flow of neighborhood boundaries based on race and ethnicity? Adam Newton locates the line between philosopohy and the social dimensions of space in Levinas's own deployment of metaphor, explaining that

"melting pot" is [Levinas's] preferred phrase to express the englobing and non-differentiating forces at work when the ethical rupture introduced by the face-to-face is lacking, when the moral particularism of the face is subsumed within a rhetoric of universalism and common transparency. . . . And while Levinas may be speaking of "ethicity" over ethnicity, the figure of a melting pot portends not just ethical loss but allegorical: faces become indistinguishable.⁷

In his epigrammatic way, Newton indicates how Levinas's philosophy of ethics includes a social or political dimension. Against melting, Levinas sustains difference. In the following, I will make clear that the aggregating ethnic categories "Jewish," "Chicano," and "black" themselves have the potential to "melt" individuals into a nondifferentiating symbolic bolus, but we first observe that in Newton's argument the boundaries groups of people put around themselves *as* groups represent meaningful modes of identification, and their too-easy erasure may whitewash the particular historical and geographical experiences that give the group its coherence and value. As *The Sellout*'s narrator knows, for instance, there is a social reality that goes by the name of "black," even as individual experience and personal particularity are not reducibale to that name. Newton is far from reifying groups of people under ethnic categories, even as he aligns "ethicity" and "ethnicity." Newton's approach to the conundrum of social identification and interethnic détente is "approach" itself, or "facing."[8] "Facing" plays off of Levinas's figuration of ethics and locates the lively charge in the verb rather than in the seemingly static noun: facing texts in comparative literature or facing locations in a study of inter-ethnic space can dislodge either object from its static formation. There is no presumed transcendent ethic that comes with facing, just as Viramontes's metaphor-as-miracle is no transcendent or universalizing intervention. Rather, the comparative work in facing—which is what Levinas is after, in the end—is the difficult practice of sustaining proximity to the other's vulnerability, especially as that vulnerability is constituted by social location. Similarly, though his register is politics and not ethics, Laclau's discussion of metaphor and metynomy suggests how an ethics of proximity can and arguably must take into account the politics of location, must be situated in, constituted by, and responsible to place.[9]

Still, if metaphor and metonymy are to meet in an act of facing— that is, in an encounter that is ethical, even as it is structured by the political—that act will have to take on the material and psychical structures of racial division, described by Moten as the stanchions of a disappeared bridge with the undercurrents of desire and the hidden economies of power flowing between them.[10] If Žižek can dismiss Levinas's ethics, it may be because the insistent priority of ethics seems to moot politics, or at least fails to take on the economic, psychical, and social forces that structure the field of ethical encounter. The assumption of a homology between mental and physical space, or between the idea of the neighbor and the physical facts composing neighbhorhoods, papers over the gap between an ethics and a politics of the neighbor. This chapter will proceed along Lefebvre's ironical tightrope to walk the boundary lines closing down or opening up neighborhoods, and to explore how physical line-making is a part of the psychical space-making of the neighborhood. As much as I have been committed in this book to synchronically and diachronically examining the physical substance of the neighborhoods in question, in this chapter I return to and turn on belief and imagination as part of the structure of a neighborhood. As with *Union de Vecinos*, the Jewish community discussed in the following sections materializes space through belief, in which religious community matters forth neighborhood boundaries.

BELIEVE IT OR NOT

The most conspicuous element of the photograph in Figure 3.1 is the fiberglass Tyrannosaurus Rex emerging from the roof of the Ripley's Believe It or Not museum, a clock gripped in its mouth, remnants of twisted metal where the teeth bit into the stand. The museum and dinosaur are the apex of Hollywood absurdism, at the corner of Hollywood Boulevard and Highland Avenue. Indeed, as Edward Soja has put it, "it all comes together in Los Angeles," especially on Highland, where tourists, locals, and the homeless encounter one another in front of the LGBT Peace Center, across the street from the Sacred Art Tattoo parlor, flanked by auto-body shops, exotic tea houses, fast-food restaurants, and seedy show-biz showcases such as Guinness World Records Museum and Ripley's.[11] Just down the street from Ripley's is the "Hollywood High 16," a set of stairs made famous in skate videos, I am told by my sons, who made me take them there, part of an international geography known only to a very select subset, and beyond the scope of this brief study. Southeast of Hollywood is Boyle Heights,

the subject of Chapter 1. To the west is downtown with its historically Mexican center, flanked by Salvadoran, Honduran, and Nicara-
guan neighborhoods. Still further west is the heart of L.A.'s Westside,
where many Jews from Boyle Heights moved after the postwar ces-
sation of discriminatory redlining housing policy. The Jews have left
their mark, with Chabad houses, Reform synagogues, and Workmen's
Circle headquarters, and lively Jewish delis. Korean, African American,
Vietnamese, and Cambodian corridors connect east and west, proving
true Soja's other claim about L.A., that "everywhere seems also to be
in Los Angeles."[12] It all comes together, but it also all flings outward;
boundaries dissolve, populations shift, and neighborhoods seem to
reconstitute every few years.

Still, circumscriptions happen, and this chapter is about the production and maintenance of boundaries and the formation of neighbor relations at the crossroads of ethics and politics and religion and
the public sphere. A closer look at the photo of the T-Rex (Figure 3.2)
reveals a subtle line, and the subject of this chapter, the material substance of a belief community.

The line is barely visible cutting across T-Rex's face, and the fact that
it does *not* call attention to itself suggests that it is part of another venture
entirely. It is the boundary wire marking the L.A. Eruv, a space which,

FIGURE 3.1 Ripley's Museum, Hollywood. Photo by Dean Franco.

according to Jewish law, is marked off as something like a domestic courtyard, allowing mundane practices otherwise prohibited as "work" on the Sabbath. The L.A. Eruv covers an enormous area, and uses some of L.A.'s heaviest trafficked freeways (the 10, the 405, and the 101) as the nominal walls of the courtyard, and this boundary wire on Highland is a *lehi* or doorway. All told, the L.A. Eruv covers eighty square miles and several economically distinct and racially diverse neighborhoods, as well as quite a few Jewish synagogue communities. The Hebrew word *eruv* translates as "mixture," and it achieves several sorts of combinations, from the mixing of public and private spaces into a single courtyard, to the mixture of Jewish and non-Jewish space, bound together in the eruv's borders, to the mixture of different groups of Jews into a single eruv community. The mixture of Jews is symbolized by the baking of a loaf of bread for which all members of the community contribute (in the form of ingredients, or through financial contribution).

The space of the L.A. Eruv is too large to be conventionally considered a neighborhood, and it covers territory not generally regarded as "Jewish" (and importantly, it is distinct from the Pico-Robertson

FIGURE 3.2 Eruv wire. Photo by Dean Franco.

Eruv, which does encircle more characteristically Jewish neighborhoods of the Westside). Of course, L.A. is not typically thought of as
a city of traditionally stable ethnic neighborhoods in the first place,
which is why Soja turns to a theory of "localities" that are "stabilized
socially and spatially through the clustered settlement of primary
activity sites and the establishment of propinquitous territorial community."[13] The L.A. Eruv, however, challenges the very concept of
propinquity. On the one hand, Orthodox Jews tend to live close to
a local shul, for ease of walking; on the other hand, the eruv creates
a nominal community across a vast territory within which many
Jews will never encounter one another. The boundary wire creates
a fiction of proximity, but its actual mark on geography is far more
subtle. This may be why, unlike with other large eruvin in the United
States and Europe, the L.A. Eruv was accomplished with little public
protest, or even notice: it imposed little to nothing upon almost no
place and no one, and its material Jewishness remains indistinct for
those not in the know, save for the public visibility of religious Jews
on the Sabbath—noticeable, but not objectionable. In Los Angeles
in the early part of the twentieth century Jews were considered undesirable by city officials and civic leaders, subject to legalized redlining, but by the 1950s Jews were increasingly regarded as white among
Los Angeles's patrician class, and postwar Jewish migration to L.A.'s
Westside met no substantial opposition. Indeed, the relocation of
the iconic, Jewish-owned Canter's Deli from Boyle Heights to Fair-
fax on the Westside in 1953 anchored that area as the heart of Jewish
L.A. Between Jewish whiteness and L.A.'s tolerance for strangeness,
not to mention the heterotopic and protean cityscape itself, it is not
surprising that there was little public notice when the eruv was first
built, and that it still remains little known to L.A.'s non-observant
and non-Jewish populations. I am tempted to compare the unknown
L.A. Eruv with the similarly unknown agricultural district Richland
Farms, described in Beatty's *The Sellout*, with both regarded as incredible when I describe them even to Angelenos.

The eruv only permits or prohibits accessibility if you believe, when, as Michel de Certeau puts it, belief requires "the subject's investment in a proposition, the *act* of saying it and considering it as true—in other words, a 'modality' of the assertion and not its content."[14] This is why, in public and legal debates over eruvin, there is always a struggle to find the right terminology to say just what the wire is. Often the wire is described as a "symbol," standing in for the idea of a door, but symbolism conflates the wire with something unseen, some force beyond the materiality of the wire, as if the wire was something that either could be worshipped or that would facilitate worship (in the way a cross or an image of Mary might). However, the function of the boundary wire is *to be a doorway*, and if the wire is a doorway, it is simply that, as prosaic as any other doorway. Even for those who subscribe to the ritual of the eruv, the wire-as-door affords no sacred function: it is not like prayer itself, or the inscription of a prayer, something linking the sacred and the profane. Rather, the wire-as-door simply permits the carrying of prosaic objects such as keys on the Sabbath. The Sabbath itself goes on, with or without the eruv. If there is a change to the city that correlates with the eruv's inscription, it is the embodied presence of Jews, insofar as the eruv exists to facilitate easier movement, and in traditional Jewish communities, where women typically are charged with domestic duties including pushing strollers and carrying children's gear, the eruv's particular affordance results in more Orthodox Jewish women in public on the Sabbath. Much like a doorway itself, which facilitates entry and exit—and when thrown open, affords a passageway between public and domestic space—the fact of the eruv gains its significance through its use.

In Southern California in particular, walking as a form of commuting is relatively rare, especially in some of the smaller suburban neighborhoods in and around Los Angeles. I venture that most non-Jews can make sense of the sight of a Jew in a long coat and kippah or fedora; that is not so odd in multicultural California. But walking? On a Saturday morning? It is a distinctly countercultural practice, and though obviously not intended as a broadcast statement to non-Jews, the walk may suggest both differing geographies and temporalities existing simultaneously. The *effort* of the walk to shul, in contrast to the ease of a drive, and the single-mindedness of that effort, as opposed to the multitasking habit of a car drive, with radio and cell phones employed along the way, casts the observing Jews as anachronisms, beyond the usual structures of temporality that govern the busy city. In this regard, the eruv is similar to a "counter-cartography," as Lize Mogel and Denis Wood among others have described: a political map that attempts to fundamentally rethink the relation of people to place, especially through mapping practices that reveal otherwise undervalued or concealed systems of power or exclusion. In this case, a minority population remaps the city to form a network of Jewish microcommunities.[15]

As a counter-cartography, the eruv maps both an intentional, ritual community and a political community, according to Charlotte Fonrobert, because "Jewish residents are made to engage their non-Jewish neighbors ritually, a unique occurrence in rabbinic halakha [law]."[16] Fonrobert is specifically referring to the "peculiar requirement of renting from the non-Jewish neighbor for the purposes of establishing the eruv," which she concludes is about "ritual unification" between Jews and non-Jews, in tandem with other eruv requirements that ritually unify the Jews living within the community. The arrangement productively blurs the boundaries between the sacred and the secular, insofar as the renting of a citywide area achieves a religious purpose through an entirely nonreligious transaction, no different from a church collaborating with transportation planners to build, say, a driveway entrance to its parking lot. What is unique is not the cooperation but the *requirement* that a non-Jew participate in the formation of the eruv, a rule much debated in the Talmud, but which Fonrobert concludes maintains the proximate spacing that is fundamental to an ethics of the neighbor: "Simply put, the fact that the non-Jew (or the mayor, the chief of police, and so forth) agrees to the symbolic interaction ultimately reflects his or her acknowledgement of the legitimate presence of a Jewish community in the neighborhood or city."[17] More than an acknowledgment of the right to be present, the L.A. Eruv community's dependence on public officials occupies the same borderline between public and private that potentially affords either the opening or closing of the space of the neighborhood. For instance, the eruv community rents the "area" within the eruv from the L.A. sheriff, because the sheriff has legal right of entry to all properties within its jurisdiction and thus control of the "area."[18]

The eruv's reliance on public utilities and its necessary "mixture" with an official non-Jew puts it in a legal borderland, comparable to the mapping work achieved by *Union de Vecinos* and even Beatty's narrator in *The Sellout*. In all instances, private claims are made on public space, and new communities are unofficially but legibly mapped onto the physical space of the city. In *Their Dogs Came with Them*, the Quarantine Authority is the literal border between a politics of subjugation and the ethics of the neighbor, as Ermila discovers when she regards the people waiting at the barricades to her block as her neighbors. On the other hand, it is against the quasi-police authority that Tranquilina shouts, "*We'rrrre not dogggs*" in Viramontes's novel, while Beatty's *The Sellout* opens with the narrator on trial for a farcical segregation that reveals the second-class status of black residents of Los Angeles. In both instances, as with the community organizing in Boyle Heights and with Baldwin's rebuke of Schulberg over the legal maintenance of inequality, the law is an agency of circumscription and immiseration. And yet, that the sheriff's office is instrumental in securing domestic space for the eruv community is congruent with the sort of violence law propagates in other instances, due to the indeterminacy of public and private located in the sheriff's office authority, and the eruv community's utilization of that indeterminacy. The eruv wire may be thought of as something like a Möbius strip, for which the inside becomes outside, and the outside folds inward. In this case, the point of involution occurs as the eruv—the institution and not the wire per se—passes through public offices such as the sheriff's. But putting the eruv alongside these other projects reveals that even as it maps out a counter-cartography in West L.A., the L.A. Eruv neither transforms the city, as UV does, nor exposes the barriers to equality, as the Watts Writers Workshop did. Rather, the chief material effect of the eruv is to increase the desirability of the area for Orthodox Jews, which is not materially insignificant, but which recalls Soja's turn to a more technical vocabulary than the ethically resonant "neighborhood." Whatever else the eruv is, it is "built around the instrumental 'presence availability' of social power. They are control centers, citadels designed to protect and dominate through what Foucault called 'the little tactics of the habitat', through a subtle geography of enclosure, confinement, surveillance, partitioning, social discipline and spatial differentiation."[19] Thought of this way, the eruv is part and parcel of the city, and its success is a measure of its congruency with and assimilation to the city's intact, ongoing regime of spatial differentiation. As Zachary Heiden puts it, "this was not the proverbial 'writing on the wall' [announcing a massive sectarian change] but rather the wall itself," or a non-sectarian, physical marker—a door and nothing more.[20]

Eruvin in general occupy a legal borderland and have been the subject of legal curiosity and constitutional challenges, particularly because the formation of the eruv requires cooperation and permission from civic authorities. An eruv is a reorganization of space around and in dialectical relation to a human subject, while that subjectivity is inseparable from the spatial arrangement of the eruv. But that dialectical formation is difficult to align with normative legal writing about eruvin—either in support of or against its constitutionality—which imagines space and subjectivity as distinct. The following passage, from an essay in *The University of Maryland Law Journal of Race, Religion, Gender & Class*, is typical of the normative conception of space, and its critique of the eruv could just as easily be a critique of *Union de Vecinos* or *The Sellout*'s remapping of Dickens (indeed, it reads like the very sort of legal theory that Beatty's narrator lampoons at the beginning and ending of that novel):

Since an eruv converts the public space within its boundaries, including the private homes, public schools, parks and shops into private religious space and "property" of the Orthodox Jewish community, its very existence implicitly pervades every aspect of the lives of those who live within its borders. While some see an eruv as "a virtually invisible boundary line indistinguishable from the utility poles and telephone wires in the area," others see it as a personal offense that forces all citizens in the area to live within an Orthodox religious enclosure. An eruv, then, brings to the fore the conflict between two overlapping legal paradigms: Rabbinic law and American Constitutional law, specifically the First Amendment.[21]

My interest in the passage is in the incongruity between its assumptions about space and the more complicated accounts of space, race, and social subjectivities revealed in this book thus far.

As should be clear by now, no spaces within a city are blank, neutral, or even static in relation to the communities that dwell within and move through them. Rather, as Soja makes clear, space is organized across a network of power relations, in which existing topographies combine with a political economy to sustain the ruling social hegemony. This organization is typically naturalized by the everydayness of living in a city, but we can tease out how this arrangement of power works, and how alternative arrangements come into being. For instance, the quoted passage posits a simple opposition between public and private space, yet the subsequent dependent clause places private homes and shops under the category of "public," suggesting that "public" already bears a conflation with some notion of the private. This is the sort of conflation that normalizes housing markets, building codes, and environmental regulations, and further masks the controlling regimes of social value that produce this tangle of policy in the first place—those swimming pools in Beverly Hills that require Watts's deprivation, to recall Baldwin's synecdoche. Thought of this way, the area within the eruv remains a public of a sort, insofar as it depends upon a non-Jewish difference in its midst, evident in the requirement of renting area from a non-Jew. Meanwhile, the privative arrangements of the eruv are highly artificial and self-consciously cathected, literally baked into a symbol—a communal loaf of bread to which all members of the eruv community contribute. Here too, it is not simply a case of private religion dominating the public sphere but of reconfiguring of "private" and "public." In this context the eruv's public partnership and its efficacy for the community of Jews who rely upon it is not a religious imposition on a secular map but an engagement with the series of already ambiguous nodal points that compose the map of the city.

Which brings us back around to the question of the materiality of the eruv. If the prosaic wire is indeed "a minimum of 'Jewishness' in a maximum of space," as Manuel Herz has argued, it nonetheless also accomplishes a maximum of Jewishness with a minimum of material.[22] To put it another way, there is a dramatic asymmetry between the material of the eruv and what it accomplishes, and that asymmetry brings us back to the gap Lefebvre observed between mental conceptions of space and physical space itself: the eruv is far more a theory of space than it is the material production of space.[23] Walking along Highland near the Ripley's museum on a bright Saturday morning, I had to struggle to discern the wire in the glaring sun, and though when I pointed my camera upward rather than at the sites around I felt like a badly informed tourist, it cannot be said that the wire's existence affected me in any way out of the ordinary. Indeed, my behaviors were well within those of the general public all around. The Hasidic Jew I saw on the other side of the street, just inside the boundary wire . . . was he walking in "a space of enunciation" as de Certeau might put it? For de Certeau, walking maps the space, assigning it its meaning through the performativity of our behavior in it. Different from the Situationists, who would *drift* through a space to feel the magnetic pull and repulsion endemic to a city, and even contrary to Lefebvre, for whom the city is a visible map of hidden economic power, de Certeau suggests that the space of the city is continually reassembled through its many "phatic" uses, lending it plural, parallel, and often simultaneous yet exclusionary meanings. Returning to the matter of neighborhoods, does the eruv committee's circumscription of the neighborhood allow for the invention of new neighbor relations, based on a common interiority? Or, as the citation from de Certeau suggests, is it the case that the neighborhood is iterative, coming into being through its material use on the one hand, but inscribed as such in a privative language, legible only to those who can read from between the lines on the other? Making the question even more complicated is the very real possibility that at any given time, the eruv may be "up" or "down," that is intact and functioning, or broken and thus invalid. If, for instance, a wire is damaged and cannot be fixed before the Sabbath, the boundary does not pertain; the courtyard is suddenly mere public space all over again, like some scene out of speculative fiction in which a world emerges and disappears at random.[24]

This transformability is possible because the eruv is not, in fact, based in any particular material property, but rather "area," which is a remarkably fungible concept. *Property* has received exorbitant critical attention in studies of race and ethnicity, as ownership is both the root of all civil rights in Lockean political theory and the basis of a theory of chattel slavery, a point I will pick up further on. *Area* is far harder to pin down than *property*, however, as it is defined as the empty space within a set of boundaries—a courtyard or a plaza for example. Consider the fourth definition of *area*, from the *OED*: "A region with vaguely defined boundaries, considered as a unit on the basis of its character, inhabitants, geography, or relative location."[25] In these terms, *area* takes on its dimensions from preexisting boundaries and its character from its demography. Renting area to an eruv community creates a palimpsestic map, layering one area over another, a heterotopic space combined with a Jewish space. The plurality of spaces afforded by the eruv knocks the usual assumptions about private belonging in the public sphere off kilter, similar to what Michael Warner calls a "counterpublic," and likewise similar to the assertion of liberation theology and black consciousness into the liberal public sphere in Boyle Heights and Beatty's Dickens.[26] Differing from those two projects, however, is the efficacy of material spacing, or the organization of space that redirects people toward encounters with difference. In the next section, I begin to consider this fictional rental agreement of the eruv as the basis for a theory of Jewishness as property, with the understanding that *Jewish* and *property* are at least as much imagined as real, more a construct for envisioning an ethics and politics of cohabitation than a condition of Jewishness itself. That theory will be supplemented with a more immediately localized and on-the-ground context for spacing and cohabitation. This is about Jewish material space, but it is neither about Jewish nationalism nor about the splendors of diaspora. Rather, it is about an investigation of contingency, first of all, and then of the political implications of that contingency.

JEWISHNESS AS PROPERTY

In her landmark 1994 *Harvard Law Review* essay "Whiteness as Property," Cheryl Harris documents the co-constitution of the legal concepts of whiteness and property, from the end of the seventeenth century through the mid-twentieth century.[27] Harris demonstrates that the legal concept of whiteness originates as the right to hold property, including one's own labor, or the right not to be enslaved, concluding that "the act necessary to lay the basis for rights in property . . . include[s] only the cultural practices of whites."[28] As the right to property subsequently transformed legally and philosophically as a right to possess whiteness, whiteness was increasingly conceived of as a form of property owned by white people. As Harris puts it, "[T]his definition laid the foundations for the idea that whiteness—that which whites alone possess—is valuable and is property."[29] Like other forms of property, the chief value of whiteness came to be understood as a vested interest, something that must be secured and policed, and its value protected in anticipation of future returns.

Elsewhere in this book I correlate that combination of rising property equity and policing with the geographical distribution of property value and human worth across Los Angeles. If whiteness is a kind of property, it is not a stretch to think of property in L.A. as a kind of whiteness, insofar as its value is speculative, depending on future returns and susceptible to depreciation by racial intermixing. Indeed, in the early twentieth century, *Los Angeles Times* publisher Harry Chandler would refer to Los Angeles as "the white spot," and his slogan became part of an anti-immigrant campaign targeting Japanese, with L.A. residents urged to "keep the 'white spot' white."[30] This was the thinking behind redlining, perpetuated by other strategies of racial containment later in the twentieth century, so it is not hard to imagine how the neighbor becomes a figure of exclusion, with neighbors mutually invested in excluding proximate dangers. Gated communities, redlines, and border walls demonstrate how relations of recognition and belonging involve the protection of sovereign space from the intrusion of the outsider, the "third" between self and other. The eruv is distinct, however, modeling a form of possession without ownership (renting) and a claim on space without property (the area). Furthermore, in the case of the eruv's claim on area, no identity (racial or otherwise) secures possession, nor does the claim of the area shore up identity. The eruv does not make anyone any more Jewish, and the required role of the non-Jew intercalates diverse concepts of public and private, along with different cultural identities. As Fonrobert explains, the eruv is a management of space that depends upon the authorizing presence of a non-Jew, in which the ritual of renting from a non-Jew effects a "unification of the residential neighborhood 'with a difference': . . . Jews and non-Jews by (symbolic) monetary transfer . . . are all potentially part of the same project of forming a collective ritual intent."[31] Fonrobert goes so far as to argue that "in its very nature . . .

the eruv as a ritual system is about hybridity, about undoing categories, boundaries, divisions, prohibitions, the letter of the law."[32] *Law*
here refers to the injunction against doing work on the Sabbath and
the eruv's perceived workaround, but it is also indeed an undoing
of secular property law insofar as it conforms to no legal concept of
property, nor does it slot neatly into the separable spheres of the sacred and the secular. Though the majority of American Jews are not
knowingly a part of an eruv community, and though it is certainly not
obligatory for Reform and secular Jews, the eruv's relationship to territory has received increasing attention from scholars and artists who,
like Fonrobert, regard it as a "powerful model of territoriality without
sovereignty and, as such, would have much to offer to the current discussions about diaspora cultures."[33]

DIASPORA TROUBLE

Any discussion of Jewish "territoriality without sovereignty" must
take on the broader relationship of diaspora Jews and the State of
Israel, a difficult dialectic that is perennially examined, challenged,
rejected, or reasserted by Jews and non-Jews. Within conventional
Jewish organizations and philanthropies, diaspora Jewry is understood
to "support" Israel, and to ultimately rely upon Jewish national sovereignty *and* territoriality in the event that—*never again*—another
nation turns on the Jews. This ostensible ready-connection to Israel
is belied by the obvious homeliness of the United States for American Jews, though even this is complicated and compounded by the
third rail of American international politics, namely political and
financial support for Israel. Even so, there are fissures in the Jewish
American bond with Israel. Though the very term *diaspora* suggests
the dialectical relevance of Israel to Jews living outside that nation,
research polling indicates that in the twenty-first century, a younger
generation of American Jews is either less identified with Israel or
less inclined to support an Israeli government that does not actively

pursue a two-state solution. At the same time, there is a growing divide between Orthodox Jews and Reform or secular Jews over support for and identification with Israel.³⁴ Orthodox Jews are far more likely to advocate for more American support for Israel, and are more supportive of the expansion of Israeli settlements on Palestinian territory. These divides have become fractious in recent years, with some prominent Jews, including the American ambassador to Israel, David Friedman, going so far as to question the Jewishness of left-wing Jewish critics of Israel. This apparent enmity maps onto the conflicts that have occurred among Orthodox and non-Orthodox Jews in New York and New Jersey over eruvin, with some secular Jews lining up to protest the eruv, and eruv committees accusing non-Orthodox of being anti-Semitic. In either case, a complicated, nuanced, evolving relationship to Jewish space collapses into a fight over who is a Jew.

Orthodoxy is the fastest-growing branch of Judaism in the first decade and a half of this century, and it has certainly seen a rise in national prominence since the presidential election of Donald Trump brought attention to his daughter's conversion to Orthodox Judaism. In contrast to Reform or secular Jews, who have historically and persistently leaned politically left of center, especially in support of civil liberties, antiracist policy, and support for human rights abroad, Orthodox Jews tend toward conservativism. If the increased public prominence of Orthodox Jews in Los Angeles boosts a general pluralism across the city, it nonetheless has the effect of skewing public recognition of Jewishness toward one particular, and particularly small sect. In fact, the majority of Los Angeles's Jewish population is *not* Orthodox. Indeed, the Jewish population of Los Angeles has the smallest percentage of Orthodox Jews—just 2 percent, compared to 15 percent in major Northeast cities. And L.A.'s Jewish population is the nation's most diverse, with communities hailing from Israel, Iran, Latin America, and North Africa. While 83 percent of L.A.'s Jews identify as non-Hispanic whites, that is a significantly smaller percentage compared to the national Jewish population, which is 95 percent white,

and the Northeast population, which is 98 percent white.[35] As Leah
Mirakhor has observed, Los Angeles's Iranian Jewish population is the
biggest in the United States, and includes many families whose culture overlaps not with European Jews but with Iranian Muslims.[36] By
facilitating the concentration of Orthodox-observant Jews in a given
locale, the eruv has the odd function of reinforcing an optical illusion,
strengthening the visual type of the Jew as the antimodern, European
throwback, especially conspicuous in multicultural Los Angeles. This
has been the basis of the pushback of Reform Jews against eruv development in other cities, where they claim that local city officials are
effectively sanctioning one kind of Jew over another. Though it may
be the case that many Reform Jews do not know about or do not care
about the affordances of an eruv, for many others, their commitment
to Reform Judaism is precisely a rejection of the sort of legalism of
which the eruv is a part.

The sectarian controversy over the eruv plays out in terms presented in this book's introduction, and can be gathered under the perennial and perennially unanswerable question, what is the substance
of Jewish identity? Jews historically have occupied a crossroads of race,
religion, nation, and now ethnicity. Indeed, at various times and in
various places, new conceptions of all of these terms were invented
to deal with "the Jewish question."[37] Shakespeare's Shylock is clearly
written to be a race apart, as is George Eliot's Daniel Deronda. Closer
to home, the Jewish American poet Emma Lazarus—author of the
famous line, "Give me your tired, your poor, your hungry"—wrote
of Jews as both a nation, which she forecasted returning to their ancient homeland (remarkably prescient in 1883), and something like an
American ethnicity.[38] It is this protean nature, not of the Jew but of
Jewish categoricality, that makes Jewish studies an important inter-
locutor for ethnic studies, a point picked up in the Conclusion, which
advocates for comparative studies. Here it is enough to say that Jewish
ethnic and religious diversity, and the expression of differing social and
political movements through Jewishness, means that "Jewish" is both

a metaphorical and a metonymical category. "Jewish" signals both a
historical continuity—which instantly prompts the question, continuous with what?—and a synchronic, social location, where Jewishness
is defined by particular actions in particular places. Jewish cultural
memory, from the recitation of the Passover Seder to the Holocaust
Remembrance Day, is a gesture toward historical Jewishness, but the
gesture itself, ritualized and reiterated in countless different ways by
different groups of Jews, is a performative iteration of Jewishness.

   This brief discussion of the diversity of Jews under the heading
"Jewish" animates both intra-ethnic discussions about Jewish identity
and, increasingly, national discussions about American Jewish support for Israel's occupation of Palestinian lands. Ambassador David
Friedman wrote an opinion piece in which he declared that anti-
occupation, pro-Israel Jews who belong to the political lobby JStreet
are "far worse than Kapos."[39] Meanwhile, the Israeli government has
conceded religious authority to an Orthodox coalition that has increasingly undermined rights and recognition for Reform Jews. This
transnational, right-wing disregard of Reform and left-wing Jews is
not new, but its recent prominence and political power has forced
many Jews to consider the relationship between their American Jewish identity, which may be aligned with left-wing causes, and their
support for an Israeli regime that maintains a quasi-Apartheid state.
On college campuses, the Jewish life organization Hillel has caused
a rift among some Jewish students by openly forbidding its chapters
from giving support to any events or speakers that challenge Israeli
government policy. In response, students have started "Open Hillel,"
a Jewish campus-life organization that seeks alliance with all manner of Jews and supports a pro-peace alliance with other campus-life
groups. Among Jewish fundraisers and national executive organization leaders, there is widespread recrimination and mutual, self-righ-
teous fingerpointing, and though this is not a broad enough split as
to cause existential concern for Jewish Americans as a community
at large, it does reflect an enmity unknown in decades. The conflict

is exacerbated by anti-Zionist activism, especially in Europe, which regularly conflates Jews and Israel. Mainstream and conservative Jewish organizations feed into that conflation, by openly declaring that Jewishness includes support for Israel, while non-Zionist Jews seek models of diaspora that justify a Jewishness free from territoriality.

Returning to the topic of this chapter, there are Jewish communities and organizations in Los Angeles that actively campaign for the sort of neighborhoods that *Union de Vecinos* has been making in East L.A., from reduced police violence to support for truly low-income housing, and several Jews, including Rabbi Aryeh Cohen, were arrested for blocking ICE officers from entering the detention center of the LAPD in April 2017.[40] Cohen is the L.A. Rabbi-in-Residence for Bend the Arc, a national Jewish justice organization with an office in Los Angeles. Bend the Arc, of course, takes a phrase popularized by Martin Luther King Jr. and frames it in the imperative. It would be an interesting study to consider how the work of "bending the arc" compares with Schulberg's attempt to trace a line from Beverly Hills to Watts, and between the two—arcs and lines—we may also recall Fred Moten's claim that an affirmative Afro-politics of justice and a critical Afro pessimism are asymptotic, comparable to an arc bending away from a line. Jewish arcs and lines aim for "justice" and put stock in the future, in the grain of a movement established by and in relation to African American civil rights activism, while Moten's arc and line are the geometrical ruins of the past forming an improvisatory space for negotiating the present. This prompts the question, what sort of mark is the eruv? On the one hand, it effectively remaps Jewish Los Angeles within a "blue line" of belonging, but on the other hand, it is disengaged from the ethics of the neighbor described by Levinas, Reinhard, and others. Cohen's and others' arrests put in stark relief a contrasting interface with the civic authorities and raises the question as to what sort of neighborhood Jews are making in Los Angeles. Bend the Arc makes no claims upon space, and acts in the name of Judaism and not for the maintenance of Jewish practices, confronting and attempting to change the character of civic law. The eruv community, in contrast, has remapped the neighborhood with a line so gossamer thin as to affect change for no one other than Jews.

The point here is less to criticize the inefficacy of the L.A. Eruv as to consider how its boundaries, laudably porous to the point of absence for non-Jews, may have the effect of excluding or at least occluding other forms of Jewish sociality. There are multiple ways of being Jewish, and to borrow from Hames-García, there are many populations of Jews in Los Angeles for whom Jewishness is one of multiple social identities that shift, merge, recede, and expand depending on time and place. This way of being Jewish aligns with what this book has so far expounded as metonymy, when what one is depends on where one is in a given place and time. A metonymical Jewishness is composed of and stabilized by the social relations of particular Jewish communities, while a metaphorical Jewishness is based on substitution: all Jews are more or less Jewish in the same way. As Laclau helps us understand, metonymy is the basis of a political consciousness: people coming together based on common proximity to some injustice. That proximate identification, like the "open-set" composition of Santner's neighborhood, does not, or at least should not resolve into something like a community based in social identification. When it does, metonymy gives way to metaphor, in which the name of the community becomes a sign of substitution, and members of the community are defined by that membership and not by the original political claims that formed the community in the first place.

In her controversial 2013 book, *Parting Ways*, Judith Butler argues not only for a Jewishness that is poised in relation to the non-Jew, but for a Jewishness that is constituted by the other. Her ostensible project is to argue for a critique of Zionism that originates in Jewish thought, itself an effort to complicate a Jewishness that is too easily identified with nationalism, and she quickly confronts the double challenge of such a project: "Indeed, even the critique of Zionism, if exclusively Jewish, extends Jewish hegemony for thinking about the region and becomes, in spite of itself, part of what we might call the Zionist effect."[41] Seeking Jewish sources for a critique of Zionism, she considers the possibility that alighting upon specifically Jewish sources suggests that there is something unique to the property of Jewishness, a reservoir of meaning that is essential to the group. By now it should be clear that continuity and substitutability are precisely the myths of identity that this book aims to dissipate, and Butler's study of Jewishness likewise seeks an identity rooted in metonymy. Butler's path out of the tautological trap of identifying through identity is to find Jewish sources whose Jewishness is constitutively and ethically engaged with the non-Jewish other. As she puts it, "I'm trying to understand how the exilic—or more emphatically, *the diasporic*—is built into the idea of the Jewish (not analytically, but historically, that is, over time); in this sense, to 'be' a Jew is to be departing from oneself, cast out into a world of the non-Jew, bound to make one's way ethically and po-litically precisely there within a world of irreversible heterogeneity."[42] The apparent gesture to history—"over time"—is quickly discarded, as Butler presents neither an anthropology of Jewish differentiation nor a genealogy of Jewish philosophy. Instead, her claim of co-consti-tution is predicated on her decade-long engagement with Emmanuel Levinas, as well as Walter Benjamin and Hannah Arendt among oth-ers who, Butler argues, advance an ontology that is constituted as an ethical relation to the other.

Just below the surface of these theoretical engagements are more pragmatic questions about how to rethink the very difficult and tragic circumstances in Israel and Palestine. In the introduction to *Parting Ways*, Butler asks the radical (as in, root) question, "What form of pol-ity could be regarded as legitimate for lands that are currently inhab-ited by Jewish and Palestinian Israelis, and by Palestinians living under occupation?" including the Palestinian diaspora.[43] The pragmatism of the question—seeking answers to a question that truly does exist in the world—is the appropriate check against a metaphysics of recognition. Butler is not after an ethics abstracted from or even prior to politics, but one that is necessarily situated in the public world wherein we engage one another. Granted, this yields an idiosyncratic version of Levinas's ethics, but it matches the present book's interest in pivoting relentlessly between the material and the discursive situation of racial assignment. Baldwin among others understood that the apparent lacuna between a universal account of what is felt or believed to be right among people and a political response to danger, violence, injustice, and terror is not simply too wide to cross, but seems to separate wholly different forms of discourse on opposite shores. Ethics begins in individual subjectivity, while politics implies people, or even a single person, whose subjectivity is a public identity. Ethics relies on a sense of imperative, politics on an assessment of power. Ethics responds to and yields intersubjective recognition, while politics exists only once recognition has occurred, and insofar as what is recognized are political identities such as "Jew" and "Arab," political recognition may be infertile grounds for ethics (think about the many programs of reciprocity such as camps, music programs, gardening projects, and the like which exist so that people whose identities are otherwise hostile to one another may come to see that "underneath, we're really all the same"). As Baldwin tried to explain to Schulberg, proximity to the other is the grounds of love, but love begins as the reckoning with the material circumstances of the other's life.

Butler's point of entry into this lacuna is Edward Said's *Freud and the Non-European*, a book that, among other insights, posits the supposed Egyptian origins of the Hebrew prophet Moses as a radical resignification of Judaic identity, and the hoped-for basis for new thinking about a binational state in Palestine premised on internal heterogeneity.[44] Butler attempts to fortify Said's suggestion by aligning it with Levinas's ethics of alterity. If, as Freud conjectures, Moses was an Egyptian and not an Israelite, then we may think of him as a Jewish Arab, someone whose subjectivity is constituted as alterity. Butler seeks a parallel with this constitutive difference in Levinas's ethics of alterity, so that Moses, the foundational figure of Jewishness, already embodies

something like a binational identity.[45] Though it is satisfying to knock
the foundations of an identity off kilter in this way, the gesture to Moses
is finally a presentist trick that belies the effort to find prior Jewish
sources for Butler's critique. It does not matter what Moses "really was,"
what matters is the work "Jew" and "Arab" can do when installed in the
origins of Jewishness. This is especially problematic given that "Jew"
and "Arab" are *political* names. At the very moment that Butler seeks
an ethical analog, via Levinas, to a politics of détente, she displaces the
ethics of intersubjectivity with its political corollary.

Readers of Levinas know that translating his ethics into a politics
of cohabitation is challenging precisely because his ethics are so fragile,
and it is surprising to find Butler so quick to literalize Levinas's concept
of "the face" into a political identity, when it is precisely such an identity that Levinas seeks to overcome on the way toward a prior ethics
of being. Butler finds license for this move in Levinas's notorious and
oft-cited claim, in an interview, that "the Palestinians have no face."
There has been quite a bit of commentary on how we might receive this
claim and thus think about Levinas's philosophy, but at a minimum,
it indicates the difficulty of transposing ethics into politics. Fittingly,
Butler returns to Said, with his dialectic of Jews and Arabs as people
mutually constituted by dispossession and trauma, and so mutually
responsible for one another and mutually cohabitable. It's a salutary
claim but it nonetheless displaces rather than shores up Levinas, and so
betrays Butler's attempt to find Jewish sources for a critique of Zionism.
Perhaps this is Butler's point, to argue *against* Levinas, though within
his grain, that there can be no account of the self, the individual, the
"I"—any form of the subject whatsoever—that is not first constituted
by a *political* other, a reprioritization of politics before ethics.

The quandary of the relation of ethics to politics, of proximity to
spacing, of borders to lines, of conduits of access to walls of constraint:
this is the animating tension in the figure of the neighbor. The neighbor is our cohabitant, the one we can neither choose nor escape, as
the relation is always defined by the topography of near-distance in

an eruv community. Cohabitation with the neighbor assumes a near-distant otherness in the required engagement with the non-Jew, and affords the possible mingling of diverse values across a diverse range of public and private spaces. Butler takes on the ethics and politics of this mingling when she turns to Hannah Arendt's conclusion at the end of *Eichman in Jerusalem*: "[N]o one can choose with whom to cohabit the earth," a seemingly self-evident statement but one which requires a supple pluralism to augment its regulatory insistence.[46] Butler supplements Arendt's maxim with William Connolly's innovative account of *pluralization*, a process of becoming plural that is part of the ongoing social negotiation of differentiation. Differentiation, not difference: Connolly draws from Deleuze, whose philosophy does not accommodate static social groups, and who advocates on behalf of a "multi-dimensional" ethos of pluralization that promotes flows of experience across multiple-identity positions, yielding a constantly fluid polity.[47] Reading Arendt through Connolly as Butler does yields the paradoxical conclusion that Jews must become dispossessed of their Jewishness, that the diaspora is not a social project either in contrast to or in parallel with Zionism (that is, a nation without a territory). Rather, Connolly's ethos of pluralization yields a paradox: "If Jewishness mandates the departure from Jewish belonging, then 'to belong' is to undergo a dispossession from the category of Jewishness."[48] Bravely, Butler does not rely on pat valorizations of diasporic nonbelonging or innocence, but cuts to the core of Jewishness, suggesting it is the experience of pluralization.

MY NEIGHBOURHOOD

Is there a form of Jewish sociality that is dispersed from itself? Can diaspora be decentered so that the ethnicity and the "ethicity" of Jewish property are commensurate and not opposed? I next turn to a short film about Sheikh Jarrah, a small neighborhood in East Jerusalem that has been under siege by Israeli Orthodox Jewish settlers who have been evicting Palestinians and occupying their homes for over a decade. Many of the Palestinians who live or lived in Sheikh Jarrah come from families that settled there from other parts of Israel following their displacement during the 1948 war. East Jerusalem was then controlled by Jordan, through which the United Nations established a permit procedure allowing refugees to build homes in this otherwise marginal neighborhood. East Jerusalem has been controlled by Israel since 1967, and Israeli settlers have been engaged in a coordinated, legal campaign to displace Palestinians from Sheikh Jarrah since 2008. The legal maneuver includes three claims: the land is historically Jewish; Palestinians do not have Israeli permits to own those homes; and most of the houses include additions to accommodate new generations of family, for which Palestinians have received no building permits. Dozens of Palestinians have been evicted, with settler families taking their place, and the goal of the settlers is to make all of Sheikh Jarrah, all of Jerusalem, and indeed all of historical Israel, completely Jewish.[49]

The 2013 documentary *My Neighbourhood*, produced by Just Vision, is about the collaboration between the Al Kurd family, who are still battling for their right to keep their home in Sheikh Jarrah, and an Israeli Jewish resistance to the settler movement. The film features Mohammed Al Kurd, thirteen years old at the time of filming, describing his life before and after the settlers came. Settlers attempted to evict his family, and succeeded in occupying a portion of the home—the addition that his father built onto his grandmother's original home. The film shows the settlers living in the same compound as the family they are trying to evict, a bizarre, hostile arrangement, the opposite of anything like an open-set neighborhood predicated in either the love for the other or an awareness of the other's precarity. In a 2016 interview, Mohammed describes the hostile standoff between the two groups of housedwellers, which includes taunting, hurling objects across the courtyard at each other, and repeated and insidious attempts by the settlers to undermine any feeling of intimacy or privacy for the Al Kurd family in their own home.[50] Young Mohammed is the quietly charismatic star of the film, which charts his complex and growing political consciousness, along with his evolving understanding of what it means to be part of a neighborhood and a nation.

The film's other principle subjects are Zvi and Sara Benninga, Jewish siblings who live a comfortable middle class life in in West Jerusalem, raised with little attention to the violence of settlement and the usurpation of Palestinian land. Explaining his childhood nonchalance, Zvi explains simply, "If you are Jewish and you are from a good home, it is easy to lead a comfortable life in Israel," though by the time he says this he and his sister have both been arrested several times for protesting the settlements in Sheikh Jarrah. Zvi and Sara interrupt the film's initial binary of Jews and Palestinians fighting over the same territory, and the film describes how for Zvi, becoming increasingly aware of the colonization of Palestinian lands compelled him to help form what would eventually become a significant resistance movement, forcing the Israeli courts to reexamine the permit question. For his part, Mohammed explains how, at first, he made no distinction between Israelis or Jews, reasonably hating them all given his family's situation. He and his family members are taken by surprise at the growing left-Jewish interest in their plight, and the film demonstrates the protestors forming human chains around Palestinian land, forcing a confrontation with the police, eventually resulting in the arrest of several Israelis.

My Neighbourhood is short on exposition, but it suggests two useful points for critical reflection at the close of this chapter. First, there are radically different ways of being Jewish. The settlers link their Jewishness to ancient history, seeking to perpetuate a continuous Jewish presence on the west bank of the Jordan river. Their claims on space are total and absolute, yielding no room for cohabitation, let alone any merging of a plurality of public and private spaces. The settlers' proximity is terrorizing, literally moving into the home of the other whom they would displace, harassing the Al Kurd family with daily taunts and repeated small abuses. This is a territoriality *with* sovereignty, and with ethnonationalism and a teleological historicity that collapses race, religion, and nation into one self-same regulatory identity—the opposite of cohabitation. In contrast, Zvi and Sara are not simply left-wing Jews with a conscience, tolerant of diversity, and committed to sharing. Rather, according to the film's framing, the siblings' Jewishness is ungrounded prior to their consciousness of Sheikh Jarrah. It is mere identity—something inherited—and not identification—the interpellation into contingent relations. By Zvi's telling, he simply lived a comfortable life as a kid and then a teenager, until he became aware of the settler land grab. At first, he was so disturbed that he thought he might leave Israel, but then, through his activism, he became more committed to his country. The film leaves untouched the question of what form of national identification can sustain both Jewish and Palestinian cohabitation, nor is it clear what resources of Jewishness would guide Zvi through his realignment. Following Butler, however, we at least observe that Zvi's evolving identification occurs *with* Palestinians, as the film depicts him in thoughtful exchange with Mohammed. At the same time, Sara's activism and repeated arrests give fits to her father, a survivor of the Holocaust who explains to the camera that he has fear of authoritarianism, be it German or Israeli. Sara's repeated confrontation with police is depicted as both a break with Jewish history and a realignment of Jewish consciousness based on claims of human rights. For the entire family, and presumably for the other Jewish activists in the film, Jewish identity is reconstituted through its activism on behalf of Palestinian land rights.

To be clear, the realignment just described is a vision the film casts forward, and only a sketch of one at that, and is not to be taken as the subsequent reality for the film's subjects. While the Benninga family continues to protest Israeli settlement, the residents of Sheikh Jarrah still live in an awful, unjust stalemate, and the Al Kurd family still has half their house occupied by hostile settlers while the land claims stagnate in the Israeli courts. Mohammed Al Kurd, interviewed by *Al Jazeera* in 2016 when he was eighteen, explained that with his family's case stalled in the courts, international attention faded. Instead of dramatic protests staged before cameras, Mohammed's family has the daily task of enduring the occupation: "It's a dangerous psychology. . . . We are tolerating them [the settlers] and enduring them. Sometimes they spew insults at us, and we spew them back, but beyond that we don't speak to each other. We just continue with our lives."[51] This is a grim psychology of "the neighbor," and it prompts the question about the film's title, *My Neighbourhood*, a phrase assigned to no one in particular in the film. That the possessive "my" is left open leaves in place the many possible ethical and political trajectories of neighbor relations discussed in this chapter, and the perpetuation of misery in Sheikh Jarrah is enough to preclude any felicitous celebration of actual neighboring among Jews and Palestinians, even if something like that does occur. Mohammed's reference to endurance recalls that term's circulation in this book so far, from Viramontes's characters to the writers of Watts, with the common experience across all three being the experience of misery-in-place. For Mohammed and his family, activism is local, identity is rooted in material experience. Whatever Palestinian identity has formed for Mohammed over the years of his family's displacement and the subsequent battles for autonomy, it will be sourced in and shaped by place. The "neighborhood" of the film's title is perhaps not so much a felicitous space of love than it is the experience of spacing in which different people are co-constituted through proximity, an arrangement that is either killing or the grounds of a polity beyond nationalist identity. As Judith Butler puts it, "[S]urely binationalism is not love, but there is, we might say, a necessary and impossible attachment that makes a mockery of identity, an ambivalence that emerges from the decentering of the nationalist ethos and that forms the basis of a permanent ethical demand."[52]

THE WRITING AND THE WALL

In 2014, someone spraypainted the words "FREE PALESTINE" across
the mural adorning the Workmen's Circle building on Robertson Boulevard, in the heart of the diverse Los Angeles Jewish community in
the Pico-Robertson district. The Workmen's Circle is a Jewish labor
organization, founded on socialist principles by emigrating Jews from
Eastern Europe at the end of the nineteenth century. The campus on
Robertson has a long history of inter-ethnic cooperation on housing, wages, and labor practices, and the mural that adorns its building commemorates Jewish socialist stalwarts Eugene Debs and Rose
Shneiderman, as well as icons of social justice and labor movements,
including Martin Luther King Jr. and Caesar Chavez.[53] The mural is
also particularly literary, with images of poet Emma Lazarus; fiction
writers Anzia Yezierska and Isaac Bashevis Singer; and novelist, story
writer, and editor of the influential periodical *The Forward*, Abra-
ham Cahan. The mural's artist, Philippine-born Eliseo Silva, chose to
highlight the Jewish holiday of Purim, explaining that the Purim narrative is about the triumph of racial justice over bigoted intolerance,
though it is also notable that Purim celebrates diasporic Jewish polity
even as celebrants are enjoined to ludic cross-ethnic performances.[54]
All of this raises the question, what sort of Jewishness was the graffiti phrase intending to target? The Workmen's Circle mural was not
Jewish-nationalist, though the organization does support a two-state
solution in Israel. In the United States, the Workmen's Circle has a
long history of working cooperatively with other racial and ethnic
groups, and pointedly, its socialist principles are the basis of its Jewish
identity, supplanting religiosity. "FREE PALESTINE" would seem to
assign this Jewish group a monolithic identity, collapsing distinctions
among Jews and the space between Israel and the diaspora. This is the
end logic of metaphorical substitution, in which multiple and diverse
iterations of an identity become subsumed under a single sign, easily
identifiable and endlessly deployable for narrowly political and not

expansively ethical ends. If Jewishness was once heterogeneous—that is, if once there were many ways of being Jewish—and if Jewishness in Los Angeles was once metonymic—that is, specific and particular to time and place, and not transposable across history and geography—diasporic Jewishness is increasingly identified as a monolithic, nationalist enterprise. While I attribute no role to the L.A. Eruv in this particular normativization of Jewishness, I do see the logic of metaphor—"one eruv uniting the Jewish community of Los Angeles" is the eruv's motto—as participating in a discursive reduction of the variegation of Jewishness and an aggregation of Jews under one iteration of the neighbor.

The Workmen's Circle mural was eventually repainted, but not before someone amended the original vandalism with an antagonistic epithet, changing "FREE" to "FUCK." Workmen's Circle board member Eric Gordon was thoughtful about both iterations of vandalism, telling the local weekly *The Jewish Journal*, "It often does take an extreme act, a catastrophe, an accident, to awaken you to needs you didn't think you had before. . . . What are we going to do? Respond to an act of hate by saying 'F—Palestine' on the mural? So, we're trying to be responsive. We agree with 'Free Palestine.' It's not the best way to express it. We are sorry and angry that they chose that way to express it, but they do have a point."[55] Gordon's startling display of equanimity gets us very close to an ethics of the neighbor that is also a politics of cohabitation. His admission that, on the one hand, a free Palestine is commensurate with the Workmen's Circle goals, and that on the other hand, he had not previously thought to commit to that freedom through formal, iterative, and artistic gestures is an example of the sort of pluralization that Butler salutes, and which *My Neighbourhood* depicts. Jewishness, already visible staked to the side of a building in the form of a mural, is forced to acknowledge an otherwise underregarded reality that was already latently present for the Workmen's Circle community. More than just a support for Palestinian rights, Gordon speaks of being "awoken" to "needs" that the community had all along without realizing it. What would it mean for the community to "need" to support the rights of others, and not simply extract that support as an extension of ideology? Gordon's use of term *awaken* seems coincidentally parallel to its currency in antiracism communities, which speak of being "woke": not awoken to the needs of others, but awoken to your need to attend to the suffering of another. This, in the end, may be what Butler is after when she affirms Levinas's ethics through a material politics, here compactly symbolized by the evolving phrasing across a Jewish neighborhood wall, converted, as it were, from a static line to a mutable border.

The Workmen's Circle contracted the original artist Silva to restore the mural, and asked him to add a message of peace, including an olive tree and the word *peace* in Hebrew, English, and Arabic: "Shalom," "Peace," and "Salaam." The addition is a remarkably conciliatory gesture, and it continues the sort of pluralist model of cultural respect that has sustained Jewishness in public life for a century, with sectarian expressions of a common virtue, represented in the original language while signifying a common public message. Nonetheless, before it was restored, the wall was a palimpsest, similar to others discussed thus far. I am reminded, for instance, of the alleyway wall claimed and painted by local organizers working with *Union de Vecinos* with the phrase "*La Vivienda es un Derecho Humano*" (Dwelling Is a Human Right") negotiating space with inscriptions of gang locality. I am also reminded of the narrator in Beatty's novel, mocking up a sign advertising a segregated, whites-only school in the heart of the otherwise black and Latino neighborhood, a fake line of division that nonetheless made visible the more complicated lines of racial hierarchy across the city. In the first instance, the two phrases painted across the wall don't compete for space so much as testify to overlapping forms of a neighborhood. The gang inscription is clear enough, and resonates with all such totalizing statements: *we* own and control this space, and anyone else is an enemy. "*Vivienda*" says otherwise, and its inscription is a performative act, the meaning of which challenges and perhaps even alters the meaning of the gang tag. The public space of the wall, be it in Boyle Heights or Pico-Robertson, may indeed be a counter-public, and an appeal for cohabitation, even as it bears witness to the darker reality of exclusionary identification.

Does an ethos of pluralization, to recall William Connolly, really change the way people think and live, really have ramifications for the material conditions of people's lives? The transition of "Free Palestine" to "Fuck Palestine" remains within the all-or-nothing frame of identity and certainly characterizes the most common forms of identification, but I am reminded of another, even more blunt form of identification that is nonetheless a claim of cohabitation referenced in the first chapter. In *Their Dogs*, Ermila's grim statement "We're fucked" is her moment of identification with the laboring men and women of her neighborhood, and the beginning of a protest against what she observes as the "fucked-up options" for the poor women in a city organized against other possibilities. *Union de Vecinos* aims for more, better options based in human rights, which are in turn sourced in neighbors' interpretations of their base living conditions, and both examples amount to a spatial reconfiguration through identification. What if an ethics of cohabitation begins not in self-contained belonging but in the uncomfortable proximity to dispossession? This is what Beatty's narrator knows when he refuses the token prize of identifying with the nation's first black president, shouting after his antagonist, the novel's final "sellout," "and what about the Native Americans? What about the Chinese, the Japanese, the Mexicans, the poor, the forests, the water, the air, the fucking California condor?" Rather than reify blackness and take pride in symbolic black victories, Beatty's narrator reiterates a signifying chain of the dispossessed, constrained, commodified, and nearly extinct—those necessarily vulnerable under narrowly conceived regimes of property rights—and insists on his place in that chain. Refusing the celebratory identity of blackness, his chain of identities resignifies the space of California itself.

The eruv is less such a chain than it is a line, less a neighborhood than a metaphor for one. It demonstrates an ethics of belonging, territory without sovereignty, to recall Fonrobert's phrase, which remains to be sequenced with a politics of cohabitation, itself an intervention into a dialectical formation of diaspora. The starting point for that sequencing, or the slash of politics across the area of ethics, would be a return to the materiality of space. This would involve not simply a tracing of a line but a reckoning with all the borders and lines that constitute an area. Writing about social space, Henri Lefebvre insists, "[social space] subsumes things produced, and encompasses their interrelationships in their coexistence and simultaneity—their (relative) order and/or (relative) disorder."[56] Linking oneself in the chain of things produced, or rendered commodities within a broader social order, is Beatty's narrator's way of beginning to reconfigure that coexistence, of sacrificing the certitudes of metaphor (basking in the success of a racial hero) and realigning territoriality through metonymy. It may also mean reading the writing on the wall ("Free Palestine") and locating oneself in that signifying chain, or making a politics out of the contingent resignification of identity.

Writing similarly about revolutionary politics, Jean-Luc Nancy distinguishes between an impoverished concept of revolution that simply turns everything over, while everything remains the same—in which the "Jewish" in Jewish nationalism or Jewish diaspora remains the same, say—and a true revolt which "protests that existence is untenable if it does not open up *spaces of sense*; that this opening up of sense is impossible so long as what reigns instead of *circulation* is the pitiless circularity in which everything-amounts-to-the-same" [my emphasis].[57] Nancy continues with an especially suggestive idiom at the close of this chapter and the close of this book: "Revolt does not discourse, it *growls*. . . . What does 'growl' mean? It's almost an onomatopoeia. It means to grunt, bellow, roar. It means to yell together . . . protest, become enraged together. One tends to grumble alone, but people growl in common. The common growl is a subterranean torrent: It passes underneath, making everything tremble."[58] The common growl: the growling "we" of "*We'rrrre not doggggs*," the "we" of *Vivienda*. The "we" in both evocations is the same "we" that, when awoken to needs that we didn't know we had before, asks, "What are we going to do?"

LOVE, SPACE, AND THE GROUNDS OF COMPARATIVE ETHNIC LITERATURE STUDY

"Places do not make for a good starting point, since every one of them are framed and localized by others—including of course the architect's studio. . . .

. . . if you stop making and remaking groups, you stop having groups."

Bruno Latour, *Reassembling the Social*[1]

I PULLED THE CAR OVER just up the road from the freeway overpass and immediately felt out of place. There was no indication that I was allowed to park here—no marked spaces or parking meters, though no prohibitive signs either. But then, who would want to park here anyway, on this featureless stretch of Motor Avenue just north of National Boulevard, and below the Santa Monica Freeway? I got out of the car with my camera and map, confirmed that I was in the right place, and began walking toward the overpass. I noticed the homeless denizens, one under a wrap of tarp and blanket on a pallet of cardboard, another walking toward me with an odd tremor in his upper body. I passed through a doorway of odor, into what seemed like a roomful of the smell of ammonia gas and urine, and it occurred to me that I would have no way of justifying my place here, a pressing concern as a police car drove slowly by, the officer inside staring not at the homeless folk but at me as I focused my camera toward the overpass. I was vaguely aware that in recent years dozens of people have been detained for photographing public spaces such as freeways, airports, and shopping malls, which have been reclassified recently as possible terrorist targets.[2]

Acting natural while feeling foolish, I looked up at the overpass and tried to see it for something other than what it obviously was, a many-ton concrete conduit for drivers who have no interest in the place where I was standing, over which they were traveling. Was there a way of looking at the freeway that would help me appreciate it as a courtyard wall, an enclosure of domestic and not simply public space? Regardless of how I looked, I could not adjust my vision enough to see this structure as a map of Jewish space, and it occurred to me that if anyone found the overpass a private site of dwelling it was the homeless men around me, who might have walked off the pages of Helena María Viramontes's novel and whose private miseries were publicly housed here, with all the wretched refuse of their makeshift domestic lives on display.

I was looking for the L.A. Eruv. According to my map, one of its boundaries was along this stretch of the Santa Monica Freeway. Earlier in the day I had been up in Hollywood photographing the boundary wire, the nearly invisible filament strung up among light poles marking the eruv's doorways, and I was getting tired and a little cranky, not to mention disoriented by my own liminal behavior, first when looking up with a craned neck in Hollywood rather than around, and now here under the overpass. None of this felt like how I was used to being in Los Angeles, where I'm otherwise typically in a car or in some clearly defined space—a museum, a concert hall, a friend's house, or a seminar room.

Still confused and wondering whether or not I was looking at the eruv and whether or not I was within the eruv space—knowing full well that I was *not* a part of the eruv community, a point I'll explain further on—I went back to my car to consult the map on my iPad. The map showed, sure enough, the freeway boundary, but I noticed something new, a drop-pin less than one mile away for the location of the Chabad community center of Cheviot Hills. I am Jewish, but I am not observant, and I thought I could stand to supplement my understanding of the eruv with a visit to the Chabad center. Of course, that would engender another series of liminal experiences. I am confidently, competently Jewish, with no anxiety about Jewish history and community. I know my way around Jewish rituals, and find Jewish intellectual history especially interesting. I am not prone to feelings of inauthenticity around more-orthodox Jews. I know what I know. The politics of the eruv are a little different from other forms of Jewish observance, however. While Jewish outreach groups such as Chabad will go out of their way to bring non-observant Jews into the fold, driving "Mitzvah mobiles" around Los Angeles, New York, and San Francisco and inveigling likely secular (male) Jewish suspects to pray or put on *tefilin*, there is a price to pay for recognizing the Jewishness of non-observant Jews within the eruv. Jews who do not observe the eruv, who sully it somehow, particularly by carrying something in public when the eruv boundary is broken, disrupt the dynamic. Of course, in an eruv community running across eighty square miles of West L.A., the majority of people within its boundaries are not Jewish, but they are largely inconsequential for the meaning and functioning of the eruv community. Secular Jews or otherwise non-observant Jews who do not participate in the eruv community—well, they are classified as *apikairos*, or outsiders. I wondered about that as I drove over to the Chabad center, where I hoped someone could tell me where to find more sections of the boundary wire. Oddly, it seemed to me, the Chabad center was not located in a business or commercial district but in a house, anonymously tucked into neighborhood tract. This was a domesticity I hadn't bargained for, and it made my approach feel all the more awkward. If I knocked on the door of the Chabad center to ask about the eruv, how would I place myself in relation to it, as an academic working on a comparative project about ethnic neighborhoods in L.A.? As a Jew?

Driving up Motor Avenue, an impulse seized me and I passed the Chabad center and gave over to the pull of this interesting, winding, hilly road. As the road curved around I caught glimpses of downtown to the east and Hollywood dead ahead, and an un-dulating swath of Central West L.A. right before me. Ordinarily, driving in Los Angeles is a chore and a bore, but in this case, like the Situationist geographers of the 1960s, I decided to let the feel of the road direct me where to go. The Situationists, led by Guy Debord, would embark on a "drift" of a city, that is, a walk with no plan, during which the walker was ever alert to the enticing or repel-ling forces within the city itself, from street layout to alleyways to the potential for mischief, violence, or delight.[3] Here I delightedly traced the road's sharp dips and narrow turns and barely perceived the moment when improvisation passed into anticipation. Without knowing how, I knew exactly where I was, and though I didn't know a single street name, nor recognize a single landmark, I found my-self carving through the narrow streets crowded with stucco-faced, Spanish-tiled bungalows guided somehow to the driveway in front of my grandparents' former home.

How did I get there? Though I visited their house weekly with my parents, even then we pulled up from the nearest freeway off-ramp at Robertson Boulevard. The route I just took must have traced some walk my grandmother used to take me on (she didn't drive), hidden in my memory until now. Their home was now occupied by a new fam-ily who had built up and out, so that the house was like a palimpsest and my memory traced a barely discernable structural scrim beneath the new growth of another's life. This was my mother's parents' home, though she was married and moved out by the time they moved in. It was the site of many unstated anxieties and odd dislocations. My grandfather was the child of poor Turkish Jewish immigrants, and he left home when he was a teenager, eventually making his way west through the CCC. My grandmother was comparatively aristocratic, born in El Salvador to a politically well-connected Catholic family, with an uncle who was a consular official living in Los Angeles when she came to California to visit her cousins. One day, the story goes, she and her cousins were confused by bus routes, and my grandfather stopped to help them find their way, and the rest is, well, the rest of the story, though I'm not sure I could tell it. Something about the marriage—perhaps religion—didn't sit well with both families. Also, my grandfather was well known to be short-tempered and prone to grudges, and he seems to have cut himself off from his family in New York at least as much as they cut him off. Perhaps he was also the one who forbade my grandmother's sisters and cousins from coming around, for by the time I was born and visiting, I assumed I had no Salvadoran relatives in the country, when in fact I had many living throughout the greater Los Angeles area.

My point here is that my mother was a Jewish Latina woman growing up in a deracinated, non-ethnic, atheistic home, and none of these identity associations meant anything for her beyond a troublesome mix of shame and fear and a dose of financial anxiety that she carried forward into our home. Though I thought of my grandmother as an immigrant, it never occurred to me, even when I became reflective about such things, to think of her or anyone else in my family as Latina. On the other hand, my Jewishness was overdetermined. My mother met my father in New York while attending a mutual relative's wedding. My parents are second cousins, but my since my mother's mother was Catholic, my mother had to convert to Judaism in order to have an Orthodox Jewish wedding. I know a colleague whose last name is the same as my mother's father's (albeit with a slightly different spelling), and best we can tell, our families emigrated from the same small town in Turkey at the same time. Looking over ships' manifests and other records, we find a common set of given and surnames in each of our families, though the birth and travel dates don't quite add up—are we related? Or is that just how village life was, replicating itself over and over? These involuted family stories were vexing to my aim of simply fitting in as a middle class white kid in Orange County when I was growing up, but they strike me now as exactly the complicated, layered, idiosyncratic and yet somehow typical material comprised in what passes under the general term *ethnicity*.

I thought about these twists and turns in family stories as I drove along Pico through Jewish, Korean, Ethiopian, and Central American neighborhoods, considering that the regional, national, and racial distinctiveness of each likely stood in for a similarly complex web of relations, doubling back on themselves in time and place, especially among those who descended from recent immigrants as my parents did, distant cousins living proximate to each other by accident or by choice. After almost an hour of driving, I made it to the eastern end of Pico near historical downtown Los Angeles, where a revival of Mexican historiography and cultural preservation competes for space and attention with the ersatz historical "Olvera Street," and both are increasingly overshadowed and undermined by the looming real estate development gentrifying East L.A., including Boyle Heights. I turned left and drove toward Pico House, among the last properties built by Pío Pico still standing. There and at the Mexican cultural heritage center I looked at images of Pico, whose mix of Spanish, African, and indigenous ancestry seems like a neat symbol of the colonial and slave-holding history of North America. Pico's facial features would become exaggerated by the effects of what is presumed to be a hormone-influencing disease that caused uncontrolled growth, giving him an aspect uniquely irreducible to any race or ethnicity. Indeed, I could only imagine that for Pico, his "race" must have shifted amid categories, dilated or contracted in importance, and facilitated or hindered his social relations across his life, from his early years as a *Californio* officer in the Mexican army to the term he served as the last governor of *alta California*, to his turbulent post-governance years as a real estate speculator in a colonized land.

THE NEIGHBORHOOD OF ETHNIC STUDIES

Could Pico have imagined Chicano studies? Can Chicano studies imagine Pico? In recent years, the answer to that second question is "yes," insofar as Chicano studies scholarship has been increasingly attentive to a conception of place, from an early politics of cultural nationalism to a political theory of liminality, and now to the shifting grounds of Southwestern geography, including the reconstruction of regional and even hemispheric identities, as well as the various and complex interface of colonial Mexico's regime of race identity as it met the expanding U.S. regime of racialization in the nineteenth century.[4] I can think of no better character for accounting for the protean *latinidad* of Californians across the nineteenth and twentieth centuries than Pío Pico. Would Pico, whose family included significant African ancestry, be a fit subject for African American studies, or even Black studies? What about Jewish studies? If the first two categorical questions require some stretching of the fields, a Jewish studies claim of Pico seems preposterously outside the boundaries of that domain of study, though my question is prompted by the obvious relevance of space to Jewishness in L.A. The Pico-Robertson district is among the most heterogeneously Jewish spaces in the nation, and if Pío Pico would *not* be a subject of a study of that space, it points out all else that would be excluded too, including the considerable majority of non-Jews and ethnic others living in that ostensibly Jewish space. I don't intend to write a race study of Pío Pico (though I hope someone else does), and my questions about how Pico would fit in any given category are in fact questions about the malleability of the categories themselves, the boundaries of which turn out to be more like porous borders than firm lines of separation.

This book's chapters have been guided by the field-imperatives of Chicana/o, Jewish, and African American literature study, and my own desire to explore where the imperatives take us when we cross outside of fields. This should not be too strenuous an effort, at least with Chicana/o and African American studies, as both are fields formed in part to overcome the erasure of material cultures and to document the endurance of brown and black people across three centuries of European domination and exploitation. Though Jewishness is not categorically a part of that history of North American colonization and

enslavement, comparative studies typically proceed by making a space
for the comparative histories, for instance by lining up the experiences
of trauma side by side to assess similarities and difference, and to chart
representational strategies particular to each group.[5] But eventually the
field imperatives of the different groups raise some interesting, troublesome questions for the would-be comparativist, which I have discussed
elsewhere and which here I'll refer to as the asymmetry of access to the
mechanisms of representation themselves: access to publishers, to the
academy and tenure lines, and to whatever rhetorical value inheres in
racial and ethnic designations, or even whiteness itself at any given
time.[6] To risk a bit of a generality, for at least two generations, Jewish
scholars have had establishment access and considerable authority in
academia in general, save for in the field of ethnic studies, which, while
certainly not without Jewish scholars, has shown little interest in the
ethnic or racial formation of Jewishness in American life.

      Why are Jews absent—or worse—from the preponderance of eth-
nic studies projects? Consider but three recent examples. Gaye Theresa Johnson's *Spaces of Conflict, Sounds of Solidarity* (2013) surveys
black and Chicano neighborhood politics in Los Angeles in the 1930s
through the 1960s, but only briefly touches on Jews, even as Johnson
acknowledges that Jews were constant participants in L.A.'s political organizing and cultural production.[7] In his *Genealogy of Literary
Multiculturalism* (2009), Christopher Douglas leaves out Jewish literature, because, he says, Jewish writers were not informed by sociological concepts of multiculturalism, though Budd Schulberg's example
is just one of many suggesting otherwise.[8] And in *The Ethnic Project*
(2013), Vilna Bashi Treitler claims "Jews created the idea of ethnic
pluralism and constructed Jewish whiteness by propping up Jews as a
model minority and contrasting themselves against blacks who they
deemed culturally deficient [sic]."[9] Subtle and important histories of
Jewish whiteness are balled up and dismissed in Treitler's claim, and
along with them, any seeming engagement between Jewish and ethnic
studies seems similarly tossed out.

In contrast, as comparative ethnic studies scholarship remains largely uninterested in Jews, Jewish studies scholarship has increasingly explored how the complex American racial imaginary gave shape to or was even used by Jewish intellectuals, lay leaders, writers, and performers to develop an American Jewishness. The field of Jewish studies has never been more attentive to race and racialization, gender and sexuality, and hemispheric and trans-Atlantic Americanity. A rollcall of recent titles in Jewish studies published by major university presses would include books on Jewish literature and postcoloniality; Jewishness and the origins of American ethnicity; Jews and Native Americans; Jews and African Americans;, Jewishness, race, and obscenity; and Jewishness and the critique of identity.[10] For at least a decade now, scholars working on Jewish American literature consider it standard practice to know about trends in postcolonial and world literature study, and to be familiar with and regularly cite the major scholarship on African American, Latina/o, Native American, and Asian American literatures. Meanwhile, ethnic studies scholars are doing ever more comparative work, studying common and commensurate trends and alliances in the literature and political cultures of multiple identities, but seem to be unaware of the very good, recent work being done in Jewish literature study.

So, what is going on? Ethnic studies and Jewish studies entered the academy at roughly the same time in the United States, in the late 1960s, though with considerably different origin stories. American Jewish studies scholarship was largely modeled on the *wissenschaft*, or nineteenth-century German-originated, scientific model of cultural study. Though in Germany Jewish studies originated as a self-validating cultural project—an attempt to legitimate Jewishness as anything other than the precursor to Christianity, as it was more typically viewed in biblical studies scholarship—by the time Jewish studies scholarship gained academic footing in the United States after World War II, it maintained a distanced, objective method of interdisciplinary inquiry. As Robert Alter put it, writing for *Commentary* in 1974, "[T]here is . . . almost

complete unanimity among teachers of Judaica that college courses in
Jewish Studies must not in any way follow the pattern of many ethnic
and women's courses in using the classroom situation for what the new
political jargon calls 'consciousness-raising'."[11] Due to the European
origins of Jewish studies, the geographical tilt toward the east coast, its
growth through private donor funds, and the 1960s-era institutional
Jewish suspicion of the new politics of multiculturalism, Jewish studies grew up and apart from the coeval development of ethnic studies.

Largely originating on the West Coast, ethnic studies scholarship
was born out of the contentious, risky, occasionally violent political
activism on campuses, when students and faculty led walkouts, protests, and sit-ins of administrative offices to demand the creation of
new academic programs. Berkeley's ethnic studies program was established in 1969, and became the seedbed for programs and departments
of African American, Chicana/o, and Asian American studies. UCLA's
Chicano studies program, founded in 1973 in response to student
activism, was all but shut down due to state budget cuts in the late
1980s, and only revived and refunded in 1993 following a fourteen-
day student hunger strike. Similar to the current climate of campus
protest, which links campus politics with the wider political landscape
of American racialization, ethnic studies scholarship was founded in
conjunction with activism reaching beyond campus, for civil rights, a
fair trial for Leonard Peltier, UFW boycotts, and reparation for Japanese internment. In the years since, ethnic studies programs have been
continually under threat of budget cuts and political censorship, with
the Arizona state legislature attacking ethnic studies in 2010.

We should think of the field of ethnic studies as a space-making
project (and I'm tempted to argue that Jewish studies is largely a his-
toriographical project). In real, material terms, ethnic studies programs have fought for space on campus, and in terms of research,
these programs have revised the map of the United States, in order
to locate the place and movement of people of color. Ethnic studies
scholarship is about access, through which it implicitly or explicitly

critiques regimes of power: the space of the nation, the university, the canon, and critiques ideologies of exclusion in aesthetic value, gender, and sexuality. At the same time, and especially in the early days (1970s through 1990s), ethnic studies scholarship was tasked with defining or even producing its object of study, either through specific projects of cultural nationalism or through population identification, thick historiography, and canon formation. We may think of the African American literary recovery projects initiated by Henry Louis Gates Jr., for instance, but also the more localized and synchronous coeval advancement of Chicana/o literature and criticism, in which writers from both domains were often encountering each other's work amid the intersections of research, teaching, workshops, and activism.

Returning to Alter's comments, it is worth noting that Alter, a poet and Hebraist, was teaching at Berkeley when its ethnic studies core was founded, and that proximity and categorical evaluation suggests not simply a historical divergence of Jewish studies and ethnic studies, but a wall willfully placed between the two, a line of division that was similarly fortified by a generation of ethnic studies scholars who dismissed Jews as nothing other than white people, at best, and part of a hegemonic power structure invested in undermining the identitarian gains of minorities in the academy, at worst.[12] I am suggesting the non-alignment of space and history: while Latina/o, African American, Native American, and Asian American scholars were making space in the academy as a way of charting histories of the group, for Jewish studies scholars, space was already overdetermined by the historical topoi of exile, diaspora, the holocaust, and Israel. The question, then, is what if anything to do about or with these different trajectories. This book has been a study in possibility, a perhaps idiosyncratic effort to hash horizontal lines of connection across the vertical lines of difference. This may be the imperative that I draw from the field of Jewish studies itself—the spacing as facing, to recall Adam Newton—and a reader may anticipate the conclusion I am after, namely that we think of comparative ethnic studies, including both congruent and incongruent fields, as composing a neighborhood. Writing from within Jewish studies, and on an entirely different occasion, Eric Santner, paraphrasing Franz Rosenzweig, supplies this formula, which strikes me as fitting both for the version of the neighbor circulating in this project and for the kind of neighborhood I imagine ethnic studies to be: "Being-neighbor in this sense does not imply resemblance, familiarity, or likeness, but rather a kind of shared resoluteness," which in this case means the commitment to academic exploration of differentiation.

WHY COMPARE?

Bruno Latour's insight that places are made in relation to other places has been borne out by my investigation of the different neighborhoods of Los Angeles, which are themselves constituted in differential relation to each other, something Paul Beatty's narrator in *The Sellout* understands. His revival of Dickens involves not simply making new signs for the freeway off-ramps but *resignifying* Dickens in relation to the rest of L.A., making visible the hidden lines of race and class subordination on the one hand, while restoring Dickens's sense of place-in-time on the other—a vestigial agricultural zone that is continuously productive, and a neighborhood bound up in a history of racial projects organized by white power in L.A. over one hundred and fifty years. Reading *The Sellout* in relation to the Watts Writers Workshop, and in comparison with localized social projects in East and West L.A., has helped bring to light how identity and identification—race and racialization—are involved in place-making. It is tempting to align identity with the regimes of constraint observed across Beatty's book, and identification with access and flow. Certainly *Union de Vecinos* uses a hermeneutics of identification embedded in Liberation Theology to make counterclaims on space, and to visibly resignify areas of Boyle Heights as zones for the protection of human rights. But it works the other way, too: Viramontes's characters mostly do not claim racial identity, but they are identified nonetheless by a reigning geno-cidal authority. The poor, brown, and broken characters in *Their Dogs Came with Them* are gathered under the sign of the dog, an object to be constrained or eliminated by the policing authorities. In real life, the hunt for the dog maps onto the policing of the Chicano Move-ment, and the Movement itself was very much a racial identification project. Viramontes shows how racial identification involves submit-ting to or resignifying the broader historical and geographical contexts wherein race takes shape and gains meaning. This is how identification and identity work, especially as figured by metonymy and metaphor, respectively, when the possibility and mobility of the one can quickly become subsumed into the static or constrained fixity of the other. In any case, Chapter 1 and the book at large demonstrate that making place and race constitute a common project, and that places and races are made in differential relation to each other.

The complexity of racial assignment discussed here is evidenced through each chapter's deep dive into a given representation of place, and through the comparisons that accumulate among the chapters. Both are necessary. Comparative study need not obviate or ignore the specificity of any given racial or ethnic group, including that group's geographical and historical constitution, its prevailing modes of repre-sentation, and its ongoing strategies for negotiating spaces of belong-ing. Indeed, I have attempted to demonstrate that comparative study can more sharply define the objects compared, and map the spaces in between. Here we recall that the neighbor, the recurring critical motif of this book, is not simply defined by place, with neighbors simply being those living in neighborhoods, but produced through spacing. Whether chosen or not, spacing is the approach, the encounter, or the contiguous relation that invokes ethical imperatives and provokes political arrange-ments. Likewise, comparison does not simply involve lining up texts or areas to arrive at an overarching assessment, critique, or argument. Rather, comparison involves situating texts or areas in proximate rela-tion to each other in order to mark the spaces of difference, and to map the contours of similarity. In the case of a city such as Los Angeles, and perhaps true for any diverse city, a comparison of the different areas reveals the dynamism of racialization, in which Beverly Hills is forever trying to arrive at Watts, in Budd Schulberg's repetition, *and* in which Watts and Beverly Hills will never meet, in James Baldwin's rejoinder. The comparison also reveals how a politics of resistance to hegemonic racialization necessarily involves an ethics of encounter, which occurs in the spacing of the neighbor. Importantly, comparison does or should not prioritize one object or one method over the other (ethics over politics, say), but should establish a chain of contiguity, or proximate relations, in which each object in the comparison becomes more visible, more familiar, and yet more uniquely itself in relation to the other. Finally, especially when they are synchronic, comparisons allow for the fact that different, simultaneous realities, including the worlds of a given text, cultural experiences, or neighborhoods—can exist at the same time, in the same place.

Comparison across defined cultural groups or racial categories allows for the exploration of the composition of the group or category itself, indeed of just what "group" or "category" can mean. Latour's observation about the making and remaking of groups needs to be complicated: racial groups are ceaselessly reiterated through ongoing social and economic forces mobilized consciously or unconsciously by people who stand to benefit from racial hierarchy. Groups are made through boundary formation, economic containment, spatial sequestration, environmental abjection, and dehumanizing erasures of history and culture. That sort of group-making can be evaded or ameliorated; groups often rename themselves in order to garner cultural recognition, and groups reiterate their histories and spaces of belonging as alternative social projects aimed at dismantling the original group-making logic in the first place. (Indeed, "white ethnicity" may be regarded as a counter-evasion, as the mid-1970s resurgence of ethnic designations appeared to briefly evacuate whiteness of its constitutive population.) The Chicano Movement was one such project, and Black Lives Matter is another. The foundation of ethnic studies in the late twentieth century launched the academic counterformation of groups, including the reclamation and renegotiation of the borders and lines of identities, and the reclamation of the histories and geographies of groups of people that underwrite and exceed Americanization. In this book I have posited that an academic comparative project allows the exploration of that group formation, the mapping of those boundaries, and the reformation of groups on the basis of new modes of critique and new forms of polity.

The comparative mode is not unique, as noted in the Introduction. My first book on comparative ethnic literature, published in 2007, was part of a cresting wave of such studies, and more, better work that examines the simultaneity of experiences, especially for Chicana/o, African American, Native American, and Asian American populations and artistic expressions, has since been published. As Gaye Theresa Johnson makes clear, this sort of comparative scholarship has often emerged organically in response to its subject, the communities of activists and artists who engaged each other in common cause, "represent[ing] an epistemological shift that made seemingly powerless minority groups able to see themselves as part of a potentially powerful eventual majority."[13] What remains something of a novelty is the inclusion of Jews in the comparative mix, including the discussion of overdetermined and even paradoxical Jewish spaces, as well as the theoretical resources associated with Jewishness, from theories of the neighbor to a generally deconstructive approach to the foundation of race, including the deconstruction of the subject across Derrida's and Judith Butler's work, with the latter becoming increasingly Jewish-identified in recent years, even as her work critiques normative foundations of Jewish identity. Benjamin Schreier's polemical critique of Jewish American literature study, *The Impossible Jew*, argues against "Jewish" itself as an organizing category of academic study.[14] Closer to the topic at hand, Barbara Mann's important study *Space and Place in Jewish Studies* identifies deconstructive architectural styles associated with Daniel Libeskind and Frank Gehry with a more general postmodern Jewish space, where post-traumatic Jewish modernity is expressed through an urban vernacular that combines late capitalist materiality and the fragmented engagements with history and memory.[15] The deconstruction of the subject, and the conclusion that race and racialization are historical, invented, and assigned to the body could lead us to be suspicious of a work such as this present book, which insists on the materiality of racial experience, even as it explores the boundaries of that experience, including what lies beyond. To put a sharp point on it, there appears to be a significant difference between how Jews in the United States relate to both nominal Jewish space and the space of the nation, and how other minority groups in the United States relate to those same sorts of spaces, and it's important to note what is at stake in taking on this difference.[16]

But this pitting of postmodernism against race and ethnicity is a false either/or choice, dismissive not only of the material reality of race but of the way race is constituted out of that postmodern reality: race is always incoherent, two (or more) things at once, even the violation of the laws of noncontradiction, and that becomes most visible through comparisons. Postmodernism is not the surpassing of identity but the visible manifestation of the plural worlds at work in and through racialization.[17] To offer but one example, the fallacy that postmodernism and racial materialism are opposite modes of inquiry appears in Amy Hungerford's *Postmodern Belief,* a book deeply attentive to religion as an American identity, but with insufficient attention to "identity" itself.[18] Hungerford assigns Jacques Derrida the role of theologian for whom language was the visible sign of a postmodern absence at the core of postwar theology, but this particularly Yale School account of Derrida, while not wrong, fails to account both for Derrida's abiding interest in material politics and for how Derrida's thought genetically constitutes a generation of postcolonial theory and critical race theory, from Gayatri Spivak and Homi Bhabha's major works to Ian Baucom's giant analysis of racial capitalism, *Specters of the Atlantic.*[19]

Oddly challenging for the present book's investigations, Hungerford posits "identity" and "belief" as opposing analytics, and laments that the former has gained so much institutional traction to the detriment of a study of the other: "The multicultural emphasis on identity as a way of understanding and dividing on up the literary landscape has sidelined belief . . . as a topic of study."[20] What should be immediately obvious to anyone working within fields covered by that banner term *multiculturalism* is that the intellectual work done there is not a matter of "emphasis" and certainly not a simple act of "dividing." Quite to the contrary, and contrary to Hungerford's thesis and hence the exile of "multicultural" literature from her book, the development of the academic study of Chicana/o, Native American, and Asian American literatures was part of a dialectical process wherein literary authors and scholars read and responded to one another's work, building off the inspiration each provided the other. Critics summoned stories, authors believed in audiences. On the subject of belief in particular, many Chicana/o writers, to name but one tradition, chart the transference of faith in a vertical deity into faith in a community, in which the community itself is formed out of material experiences and common social values. Put more simply, Chicana/o writers and many other "multicultural" authors redirect belief toward critical practices that reach well beyond academia, linking powerfully from the 1960s through the 1980s with labor politics and civil and human rights activism. Viramontes's collected works should be enough to prove the point, but we could look to foundational literature by Ana Castillo, Tomás Rivera, Alejandro Morales, and Sandra Cisneros for examples of the literary intersection of belief and identity, and the concomitant scholarship on Chicana/o literature would bear out the critical salience of that intersection.[21]

As for the comparative project outlined here, consider that belief is directional, deriving its meaning and perhaps its capacity from its object. *What* you believe in determines *how* you believe, as well as the implications for belief. Belief is temporally disjunctive: a belief in something from the past is not the same as a belief in the present, nor are both the same as a belief in, say, a redeeming future. Between the subject and the object of belief is a sort of spacing, a proximate arrangement full of the burden of the decision, as Gayatri Spivak put it. Bernard Malamud's short story "Angel Levine," written in the 1950s when the Jewish American writer was exploring the common experiences of African Americans and Jews, features precisely this sort of belief-decision, with the character Manischevitz faced with the choice to believe that a black man from Harlem is at once a Jew, an angel, and the savior of his ailing wife. The story is not simply about what to believe in—black Jews, Jewish universality, some conventional form of cultural pluralism—but how belief is a choice. Facing Levine, who has been living in squalor since Manischevitz initially and incredulously rejected his help, Manischevitz considers:

Should he say he believed a half-drunken Negro to be an angel? Manischevitz was recalling scenes of his youth as a wheel in his mind whirred: believe, do not, yes, no, yes, no. The pointer pointed to yes, to between yes and no, to no, no it was yes. He sighed. It moved but one had still to make a choice.[22]

The choice is a decision, and the root of that word (to cut, as with scissors) reminds us that it implies a commitment, cutting off all other possible choices once made. But what is decided, or what is the implication of believing? Neither in this story nor in the story I am telling about multiracial Los Angeles is belief in the other a simple assimilation to the self, nor is it any easy obviation of the differing experiences of racialization. Leaning on etymology further still, we note that *belief* is rooted in the word *love*, signifying something like "in-love" or committed to the love of something, and recalling Badiou's Lacanian suggestion that love is the act of spacing which makes an ethics of the neighbor possible, we may say that Malamud's story about belief is likewise a story about the neighbor, in which the contingencies of racialization matter, regardless of the inclination of postmodernist critics who wished it did not.[23]

It occurred to me to think about the spatial relations among the characters of "Angel Levine" only after I had read Viramontes's *Their Dogs Came with Them*, and the particular sociological encounter afforded by belief in Malamud's story came into relief in comparison with belief's shattering effect for Tranquilina and indeed for the reader at the end of *Their Dogs*. There is, in fact, the intimation of flight at the end of both stories, with Levine getting his angel's wings and buzzing skyward, presumably to heaven. The ascendance is perhaps cartoonish, as if the story does not entirely believe in its own centering of the supernatural within the category of belief, and so the final line, "believe me . . . there are Jews everywhere," with its colloquial use of "believe" and its emphasis on material space, redirects the story's energy back to comparative geography. The universality of "everywhere" can only begin with a comparison of the Lower East Side and Harlem. The optimism of Malamud's story is, of course, in stark contrast to the violence and death that close Viramontes's novel, when even the most hopeful reader who puts stock in Tranquilina's faith—believes in her belief—must acknowledge that belief is not a final commentary on circumstances but at best the beginning of an ethical and political stance taken up on behalf of the residents of Boyle Heights. The grim realism of *Their Dogs* does not cancel out "Angel Levine," of course, but the difference between the two does cancel out any simple claims one might make about race and space, or about how belief can moot how race materializes for different people in different places. This book has sought not to bridge over difference with metaphor but to dwell in the space between two proximate subjects and measure the near distance between them. Dwelling between neighborhoods, narratives, and cultures means experiencing the torsion of borders pressed against each other, and hearing the chilling call of the different "growls." Dwelling in that space, pursuing ever better accounts of such constitutions and even co-constitutions of identities, is the dizzying, dispossessing love of comparative ethnic literature study.

NOTES

INTRODUCTION: The Borders and Lines of Social Identities

1. Jonathan Gold, "The Year I Ate Pico Boulevard," *LA Weekly*, September 23, 1998, http://www.laweekly.com/news/the-year-i-ate-pico-boulevard-2129883.

2. Michael Omi and Howard Winant, *Racial Formation in the United States, from the 1960s to the 1980s*. 2nd ed. (New York: Routledge, 1992), 65–66.

3. Gaye Theresa Johnson, *Spaces of Conflict, Sounds of Solidarity: Music, Race, and Spatial Entitlement in Los Angeles* (Berkeley: University of California Press, 2013), 15.

4. Ibid., 1.

5. See Helena María Viramontes, *Their Dogs Came with Them* (New York: Atria Books, 2007); Paul Beatty, *The Sellout* (New York: Farrar, Straus and Giroux, 2015); Budd Schulberg, ed., *From the Ashes: The Voices of Watts* (New York: Meridian, 1969).

6. This is Mark Wild's analysis in his monograph *Street Meeting: Multiethnic Neighborhoods in Early Twentieth-Century Los Angeles* (Los Angeles: University of California Press, 2005).

7. See Walter Benn Michaels, *Our America: Nativism, Modernism, and Pluralism* (Durham, NC: Duke University Press, 1995); Paul Gilroy, *Against Race: Imagining Political Culture Beyond the Color Line* (Cambridge, MA: Harvard University Press, 2000); Mark Lilla, *The Once and Future Liberal: After Identity Politics* (New York: HarperCollins, 2017).

8. See Lisa Lowe, *Immigrant Acts: On Asian American Cultural Politics* (Durham, NC: Duke University Press, 1996); Johnella Butler, *Color-Line to Borderlands: The Matrix of American Ethnic Studies* (Seattle: University of Washington Press, 2001); Arturo J. Aldama, *Disrupting Savagism: Intersecting Chicana/o, Mexican Immigrant, and Native American Struggles for Self-Representation* (Durham, NC: Duke University Press, 2001).

9. On African American literature's hemispheric dimension, see Judith Madera, *Black Atlas: Geography and Flow in Nineteenth Century African American Literature* (Durham, NC: Duke University Press, 2015). On hemispheric Latina/o writing, see Paula M. L. Moya and Ramón Saldívar, "Fictions of the Trans-American Imaginary," *Modern Fiction Studies* 49, no. 1 (2003): 1–18, https://doi.org/10.1353/mfs.2003.0007.

10. Louis Althusser, "Ideology and the Ideological State Apparatuses (Notes Toward an Investigation)," in *Lenin and Philosophy and Other Essays* (New York: Verso, 1970), 11.

11. María Josefina Saldaña-Portillo. *Indian Given: Racial Geographies Across Mexico and the United States.* (Durham, NC: Duke University Press, 2016), 17.

12. Beatty, *The Sellout*.

13. See Hannah Arendt, *Love and Saint Augustine*, ed. Joanna Vecchiarelli Scott and Judith Chelius Stark (Chicago: University of Chicago Press, 1998); Emmanuel Levinas, "Peace and Proximity," in *Basic Philosophical Writings*, ed. Adriaan T. Peperzak, Simon Critchley, and Robert Bernasconi (Bloomington: Indiana University Press, 1996), 161–170.

14. Slavoj Žižek, Eric L. Santner, and Kenneth Reinhard, *The Neighbor: Three Inquires in Political Theology* (Chicago: University of Chicago Press, 2005).

15. See Carlos Manuel Salomon, *Pío Pico: The Last Governor of Mexican California* (Norman: University of Oklahoma Press, 2010).

16. Ibid.

17. See Mike Davis, *City of Quartz: Excavating the Future in Los Angeles* (New York: Verso, 2006).

18. Chester Himes, *If He Hollers, Let Him Go* (New York: DeCapo, 2002).

19. Elizabeth Povinelli, *Economies of Abandonment: Social Belonging and Endurance in Late Liberalism* (Durham, NC: Duke University Press, 2011), 134.

20. I am aware that my book leaves out many racial groups important to the story of Los Angeles, including Asian Americans. The stories of Chinese- and Japanese-descent residents of Los Angeles are indispensable for understanding racial formation in the city, and Korean Americans were very much at the center of the complex racial imaginary throughout the late twentieth century. The absence of those stories here is not the result of unintentional neglect but simply respect for the importance of field expertise. I am not an expert in those histories, nor do I have expertise on the multiple dimensions of Asian American racialization. For an excellent recent book on Southern California and Asian racialization, see Karen Tongson, *Relocations: Queer Suburban Imaginaries* (New York: New York University Press, 2011).

21. *The Daily Show with Jon Stewart*, "Barack Obama," Comedy Central, September 10, 2008, written by Rory Albanese and Kevin Bleyer, directed by Chuck O'Neil, http://www.cc.com/video-clips/277mp5/the-daily-show-with-jon-stewart-barack-obama.

22. Michael Hames-García, *Identity Complex: Making the Case for Multiplicity* (Minneapolis: University of Minnesota Press, 2011), ix.

23. Ibid., 6.

24. Paula M. L. Moya, *Learning from Experience: Minority Identities, Multicultural Struggles* (Los Angeles: University of California Press, 2002), 13.

25. Mary Pat Brady, *Extinct Lands, Temporal Geographies: Chicana Literature and the Urgency of Space* (Durham, NC: Duke University Press), 7.

26. Rashad Shabazz, *Spatializing Blackness: Architectures of Confinement and Black Masculinity in Chicago* (Urbana: University of Illinois Press, 2015), 2.

27. Barack Obama, "Remarks by the President on Trayvon Martin," Office of the Press Secretary, the White House, July 19, 2013, https://obamawhitehouse .archives.gov/the-press-office/2013/07/19/remarks-president-trayvon-martin.

28. Ernesto Laclau, *The Rhetorical Foundations of Society* (New York: Verso, 2014), 60.

29. Ibid., 63.

30. See Jacques Rancière, "Wrong: Politics and Police," in *Disagreement: Politics and Philosophy*, trans. Julie Rose (Minneapolis: University of Minnesota Press, 2004).

31. Elizabeth Anker steered me to Laclau's text, though I credit her with more than a simple book recommendation. Among the most generous of colleagues, she spent patient hours reading my work and listening to me explain my thinking, and the Laclau recommendation is only the most tangible mark that her generosity has had on this project.

32. Laclau, *Rhetorical Foundations*, 68.

33. See Viramontes, *Their Dogs Came with Them*.

34. Américo Paredes, *With His Pistol in His Hand: A Border Ballad and Its Hero* (Austin: University of Texas Press, 1958).

35. Jeremy Raff, "The No Man's Land Beneath the Border Wall," *Atlantic Monthly* documentary, July 7, 2016, https://www.theatlantic.com/video/ index/490241/in-texas-stuck-on-mexican-side-of-the-border-wall.

36. Gloria Anzaldúa, *Borderlands/La Frontera* (San Francisco: Aunte Lute Books, 1987), Preface.

37. Sandro Mezzadra and Brett Neilson, *Border as Method: Or, the Multiplication of Labor* (Durham, NC: Duke University Press, 2013), 7.

38. Caroline Levine, *Forms: Whole, Rhythm, Hierarchy, Network* (Princeton, NJ: Princeton University Press, 2015), 118.

39. Ibid., 119.

40. Writing about "urban renewal" projects, for instance, K. Ian Grandison argues, "the bleeding wound of the freeway erects a racial barricade to resist the mixing of black and white and to exclude the mass of African Americans from accessing the political, social, and economic resources of full citizenship." "The Other

Side of the 'Free' way: Planning for 'Separate But Equal' in the Wake of Massive Resistance," in *Race and Real Estate*, ed. Adrienne Brown and Valerie Smith (New York: Oxford University Press, 2015), 207.

41. See Schulberg, *From the Ashes*.

42. See James Baldwin, *The Fire Next Time* (New York: Vintage, 1993) and *No Name in the Street* (New York: Vintage, 2007).

43. *My Neighborhood*, directed by Julia Bacha and Rebekah Wingert-Jabi (2010: Just Vision).

CHAPTER 1: Redlining and Realigning in East L.A.

1. Franz Rosenzweig, *The Star of Redemption*, trans. Barbara E. Galli (Madison: University of Wisconsin Press, 2005).

2. See Sarah Imhoff, *Masculinity and the Making of American Judaism* (Bloomington: Indiana University Press, 2017).

3. See Isabel Wilkerson, "Aftermath," in *The Warmth of Other Suns: The Epic Story of America's Great Migration* (New York: Vintage, 2010).

4. Thomas Claviez, "Done and Over With—Finally?: Otherness, Metonymy, and the Ethics of Comparison," *PMLA*, 128, no. 3 (May 2013): 608–614.

5. See Dean Franco, *Race, Rights, and Recognition: Jewish American Literature Since 1969* (Ithaca, NY: Cornell University Press, 2012).

6. See Richard Rorty, *Contingency, Irony, and Solidarity* (New York: Cambridge University Press, 1989).

7. Helena María Viramontes, *Their Dogs Came with Them* (New York: Atria Books, 2007), 236.

8. I offered my interpretation of this passage to Viramontes herself. She confirmed that she hoped the flowers would call Mary to mind, and she also affirmed that she only *hoped* the reader would see it—that she didn't want to over-draw the picture. I offer this here not to say "I'm right" but to underscore the problem of locating the metaphor, including metaphor's dependence on interpretive stance.

9. Here I acknowledge the allusion in my title, a paraphrase of Eric L. Santner's essay "Miracles Happen: Benjamin, Rosenzweig, Freud, and the Matter of the Neighbor," in Slavoj Žižek , Eric L. Santner, and Kenneth Reinhard, *The Neighbor: Three Inquires in Political Theology* (Chicago: University of Chicago Press, 2005). Though not directly cited here, Santner's work has been especially influential for my coming to terms with the intrusion of miracle into the secular world, including the dynamics of desire associated with receptivity. In addition to "Miracles Happen," see Santner's *On The Psychotheology of Everyday Life: Reflections on Freud and Rosenzweig* (Chicago: University of Chicago Press, 2001).

10. See Gilles Deleuze, *Bergsonism*, trans. Hugh Tomlinson and Barbara Habberjam (New York: Zone Books, 1991); Elizabeth Grosz, *Becoming Undone: Darwinian Reflections on Life, Politics, and Art* (Durham, NC: Duke University Press,

2011); Jane Bennett, *Vibrant Matter: A Political Ecology of Things* (Durham, NC: Duke University Press, 2010); Bruno Latour, *Reassembling the Social: An Introduction to Actor-Network Theory* (New York: Oxford University Press, 2007).

11. See, for instance, Zamora and Faris's canonical introduction to *Magical Realism: Theory, History, and Community* (Durham, NC: Duke University Press, 1995).

12. Gayatri Chakravorty Spivak, *An Aesthetic Education in the Era of Globalization* (Cambridge, MA: Harvard University Press, 2013), 109.

13. With a very different sort of reading, Juan D. Mah y Busch also alights on the efficacy of metaphor for love in his essay "Lovingly: Ethics in Viramontes's Stories" in *Rebozos de Palabras: An Helena Maria Viramontes Critical Reader* (Tucson: University of Arizona Press, 2013). See also Mary Pat Brady's exceptionally important historicist essay, which also regards metaphor, "Metaphors to Love By: Toward a Chicana Aesthetics in *Their Dogs Came with Them*" in the same volume.

14. William James's essay "The Will to Believe" is the referent here, and though it seems a far step from Santner, not to mention Deleuze and Guattari cited later on, this essay's claim is that the sort of pragmatic world-making that James describes (and that Deleuze, especially, engages through his work on Bergson) is consonant with the logic of "the thing/inside the thing" in Santner's and Reinhard's essays engaging the philosophy of Alain Badiou. William James, "The Will to Believe," in *William James Writings 1878–1899* (New York: Library of America, 1992).

15. See Immanuel Kant, *Observations on the Feeling of the Beautiful and Sublime*, 2nd ed., trans. John T. Goldthwait (Berkeley: University of California Press, 2004); Friedrich Nietzche, *On the Genealogy of Morality*, trans. Maudemarie Clark and Alan J. Swensen (Indianapolis: Hackett, 1998); Jacques Derrida, "Structure, Sign, and Play in the Discourse of the Human Sciences," in *Writing and Difference*, trans. Alan Bass, rep. ed. (Chicago: University of Chicago Press, 1978), chap. 10; Paul de Man, *Blindness and Insight: Essays in the Rhetoric of Contemporary Criticism*, 2nd ed. (Minneapolis: University of Minnesota Press, 1983).

16. Kenneth Burke, *A Grammar of Motives* (New York: Prentice Hall, 1945), 503–504.

17. See Rorty, *Contingency, Irony, and Solidarity*.

18. Roman Jakobson, *On Language* (Cambridge, MA: Harvard University Press, 1995. It is important to recall that while Jakobson clearly associates romantic and realist literature with metaphor and metonymy respectively, he closes his chapter on aphasia with a cheeky reminder that the two operations of language are in fact part of a bipolar system and that it is literary critics who in fact have—aphasia-like—neglected to see the cooperation of metonymy in metaphorical sign systems (132–133).

19. The Moratorium was an organized protest against the Vietnam War that made effective use of the city's parks, including Obregan and Salazar Parks, both centrally located though never mentioned in the space of the novel. See F. Arturo Rosales, *Chicano: The History of the Mexican American Civil Rights Movement* (Houston: Arte Publico, 1997), 200.

20. See Miguel Leon-Portilla, *The Broken Spears: The Aztec Account of the Conquest of Mexico*, 2nd ed., trans. Lysander Kemp (Boston: Beacon Press, 2006).

21. See Viramontes's "Interview" with Michael Silverblatt, https://www.kcrw.com/news-culture/shows/bookworm/helena-maria-viramontes.

22. Gayatri Spivak puts it this way: "The most pervasive double bind undoes the individual-collective dichotomy by way of a thinking, of death, that would undo the human-animal dichotomy as well." See Spivak, *An Aesthetic Education in the Era of Globalization*, 30.

23. See Latour, *Reassembling the Social*.

24. See Hsuan Hsu, "Fatal Contiguities: Metonymy and Environmental Justice," *New Literary History* 42, no. 1 (Winter 2011), 147–168, https://doi:10.1353/nlh.2011.0007.

25. Hsu, "Fatal Contiguities," 159; Viramontes, *Their Dogs*, 125.

26. Hsu observes the ubiquity of "Ben-like people" but does not credit the possibility that Tranquilina, too, reads the substitutability of Ben as metaphorical. See Hsu, "Fatal Contiguities," 159.

27. Emmanuel Levinas, "Peace and Proximity," in *Emmanuel Levinas: Basic Philosophical Writings*, ed. Adriaan T. Peperzak, Simon Chritchley, and Robert Bernasconi (Bloomington: Indiana University Press, 1996).

28. Rosi Braidotti, *Transpositions: On Nomadic Ethics* (Malden, MA: Polity, 2006), 234.

29. See Deleuze, *Bergsonism*.

30. This phrasing is borrowed from William E. Connolly's book *Worlds of Becoming* (Durham, NC: Duke University Press, 2011).

31. See Tina Sussman, "Devout See Virgin Mary in N.J. Tree Trunk, Erect Shrine Around It," *Los Angeles Times*, July 13, 2012, accessed February 16, 2018, http://articles.latimes.com/2012/jul/13/nation/la-na-nn-virgin-tree-20120713.

32. Gilles Deleuze and Felix Guattari, *A Thousand Plateaus: Capitalism and Schizophrenia*, trans. Brian Massumi (Minneapolis: University of Minnesota Press, 1987), 3.

33. See, for instance, Helena María Viramontes, *The Moths and Other Stories* (Houston: Arte Publico, 1995).

34. Žižek, Santner, and Reinhard, *The Neighbor*, 28.

35. Santner, *On the Psychotheology of Everyday Life*, 8.

36. Žižek, Santner, and Reinhard, *The Neighbor*, 66.

37. Ibid., 67.

38. Ibid., 68.

39. Alain Badiou, *Ethics: An Essay on the Understanding of Evil*, trans. Peter Hallward (New York: Verso, 2013), 52.

40. Elizabeth Grosz, *Becoming Undone*, 55.

41. Latour might say Ulysses is "other-taken," his phrase (alternative to "overtaken") for how we can be reoriented not through some generic force of power, but through material and psychological networks that are complicated but nonetheless traceable and that novels in particular are apt to represent See *Reassembling the Social*, 45.

42. See Slavoj Žižek, "Smashing the Neighbor's Face," Lacan Dotcom, 1997/2005, http://www.lacan.com/zizsmash.htm.

43. Not exactly like Agamben's account of the *Musselmann* in *Remnants of Auschwitz*, the walking dead of the Nazi concentration camps, Viramontes's ending nonetheless similarly seeks the borderline between human and inhuman that inheres in ecologies of exhaustion and deprivation. See Giorgio Agamben, *Remnants of Auschwitz: The Witness and the Archive*, trans. Daniel Heller-Roazen (New York: Zone Books, 2002).

44. Pheng Cheah, *Inhuman Conditions: On Cosmopolitan and Human Rights* (Cambridge, MA: Harvard University Press, 2007), 180.

45. Jacques Rancière, *Disagreement: Politics and Philosophy*, trans. Julie Rose (Minneapolis: University of Minnesota Press, 1999), 30.

46. Hsu believes she dies and reads the end as clearly tragic, the end of possibility. Obviously, I disagree. See Hsu, "Fatal Contiguities," 163.

47. Badiou, *Ethics*, 115.

48. Spivak, *An Aesthetic Education in the Era of Globalization*, 23.

49. I acknowledge that for Spivak the human impulse to figure the aporetic is the attempt to domesticate it. I don't exactly disagree so much as I think "the human" is transfigured in the very act of figuration, increasing and not decreasing strangeness.

50. Eric Hayot prompts my question with his thesis that "aesthetic worlds, no matter how they form themselves, are among other things, always relations to and theories of the lived world, whether as largely unconscious normative constructs, as rearticulations, or even as active refusals of the world-norms of their age." Eric Hayot, *On Literary Worlds* (New York: Oxford University Press, 2012), 137.

51. Bonnie Honig, *Emergency Politics: Paradox, Law, Democracy* (Princeton, NJ: Princeton University Press, 2009), 84–85.

52. Ibid., 86.

53. Helena María Viramontes, "Scripted Language: Writing Is the Only Way I Know How to Pray," talk given at Cornell University, November 11, 2009, posted June 17, 2010, http://www.cornell.edu/video/helena-viramontes-scripted-language.

54. At the same time that I am reciting Spivak's words from the beginning of this essay, I harmonize with Elizabeth Povinelli's conclusion of *Economies of Abandonment*: "The imprint these social worlds have made on my work is not a pure copy of their worlds. . . . These are tracings that will then be traced. All of these tracings are the prehistory of a new positive form of life even as they are the conditions for 'not this' and 'not that'." Elizabeth Povinelli, *Economies of Abandonment: Social Belonging and Endurance in Late Liberalism* (Durham, NC: Duke University Press, 2011), 192.

55. Paula Moya, *The Social Imperative: Race, Close Reading, and Contemporary Literary Criticism* (Stanford, CA: Stanford University Press, 2016), 165.

56. See the chapter titled "Critique of Violence" in Walter Benjamin, *Reflections: Essays, Aphorisms, Autobiographical Writings*, ed. Peter Demetz (New York: Schocken, 1986).

57. See Benjamin's "Critique of Violence" in *Reflections* and Judith Butler's commentary from *Parting Ways: Jewishness and the Critique of Zionism* (New York: Columbia University Press, 2012).

58. All of my knowledge of *Union de Vecinos* comes from several conversations with its founding co-director, Leonardo Vilchis. Over a three-year period, Leonardo was generous enough to spend full days with me, both in his office on Fickett street in Boyle Heights and through meandering drives and walks across the area. Frequently, we would stop and speak with neighbors to hear their stories, and Leonardo would tell me about the recent histories of the various spaces—buildings, alleyways, intersections, street corners. As I write this, *Union de Vecinos* is engaged in a new battle, not against gangs or violent policing, but with the capitalist takeover of Boyle Heights by international developers.

59. Kristien Justaert, "Cartographies of Experience: Rethinking the Method of Liberation Theology," *Horizons* 42, no. 2 (December 2015): 245, https://doi.org/10.1017/hor.2015.59. The full quote includes a dismissal of "the face," Levinas's figure for ethics. I elided Justaert's line simply because it was not relevant to the point, but here I note it both to represent her thought and to critique it. Judith Butler among others has adequately demonstrated that Levinas's face is perfectly appositional with an embodied ethics. See Butler, *Precarious Life: The Powers of Mourning and Violence* (New York: Verso, 2004).

60. Justaert, "Cartographies," 245.

61. Michel Foucault, *Language, Counter-Memory, Practice: Selected Essays and Interviews* (Ithaca, NY: Cornell University Press, 1980), 206.

CHAPTER 2: The Matter of the Neighbor and the Property of "Unmitigated Blackness"

1. Fred Moten, "Blackness and Nothingness (Mysticism in the Flesh)," *The South Atlantic Quarterly* 112, no. 4 (Fall 2013): 778.

2. Keeanga-Yamahtta Taylor, *From Black Lives Matter to Black Liberation* (Chicago: Haymarket, 2016), 192.

3. See, for instance, the statement on restorative justice by the Black Lives Matter collective. "We Affirm That All Black Lives Matter," Black Lives Matter, accessed August 31, 2017, http://blacklivesmatter.com/guiding-principles.

4. J. L. Austin, *How to Do Things with Words*, 2nd ed. (Cambridge, MA: Harvard University Press, 1975). Curiously, the Oxford English Dictionary suggests that the verb form of *matter* is typically used in negative and interrogative contexts, that is, to dismiss something that does *not* matter. This reversal—the negation of a negation—also gives the phrase its rhetorical force and renders moot the knee-jerk reaction, "*all* lives matter," which is already a performance of democracy's elision of material inequality. Instead, "Black Lives Matter" elides the long-implied negative, "black lives *do not* matter"; saying it, you admit that black people suffer the material consequences of white supremacy, and you commit to a version of democracy that begins with the acknowledgment of racial violence. *OED Online*, s.v. "matter (v.)," accessed September 12, 2017, http://www.oed.com /view/Entry/115085?rskey=XIi6df&result=3&isAdvanced=false.

5. See, for instance, Gregory S. Jay, *American Literature and the Culture Wars* (Ithaca, NY: Cornell University Press, 1997); Donald Pease, ed., *National Identities and Post-Americanist Narratives* (Durham, NC: Duke University Press, 1994).

6. See, for example, Ta-Nehisi Coates, *Between the World and Me* (New York: Random House, 2015).

7. Writing about the construction of freeways in Richmond, Virginia, K. Ian Grandison describes the freeway as "a racial weapon to put African-Americans, and their dreams for inclusive citizenship, back in their proper place. Either obliterated by the freeway, or pressed up against it through the glaring disrespect for their homes and institutions, African Americans were being told in the most flagrant way imaginable that, despite hopeful new interpretations of civil rights law, they still did not belong on the right side of the tracks." "The Other Side of the 'Free' Way: Planning for 'Separate But Equal' in the Wake of Massive Resistance," in *Race and Real Estate*, ed. Adrienne Brown and Valerie Smith (New York: Oxford University Press, 2015), 221.

8. Joshua Clover, *Riot, Strike, Riot: The New Era of Uprisings* (New York: Verso, 2016), 182. Meanwhile, several state legislatures have drafted bills that would defer prosecution of drivers who run down pedestrian protestors in the streets, thereby affirming that the material dimensions of protest have a metaphorical corollary, too: flows of capital and power are being prioritized over political interruption. See Colin Campbell, "Drivers Who Hit Protestors Blocking Roads Could Be Protected Under NC House Bill," *The News & Observer*, April 26, 2017, http://www.newsobserver.com/news/politics-government/state-politics /article146957349.html.

9. See Elizabeth Povinelli, *Economies of Abandonment: Social Belonging and Endurance in Late Liberalism* (Durham, NC: Duke University Press, 2011).

10. See Povinelli, *Economies of Abandonment*, 133.

11. Budd Schulberg, *From the Ashes: Voices of Watts* (New York: Meridian Books, 1967).

12. Daniel Widener, *Black Arts West: Culture and Struggle in Postwar Los Angeles* (Durham, NC: Duke University Press, 2010), 108.

13. This is the FBI plant Darthard Perry's own account. "Cointelpro Documentary, Part 4 of 6 (FBI Informant Confesses That FBI Had Him Commit Arson)," YouTube video, 9:24, posted by atgbf1397, October 23, 2009, https://www.youtube.com/watch?v=UHnUFpCeGxQ.

14. See Budd Schulberg, *What Makes Sammy Run* (New York: Vintage, 1993); Budd Schulberg, *The Disenchanted* (Minneapolis: University of Minnesota Press, 2012); Budd Schulberg, *The Harder They Fall* (Chicago: Ivan R. Dee, 2007); *On the Waterfront*, directed by Elia Kazan, written by Budd Schulberg (Horizon Pictures, 1954); *A Face in the Crowd*, directed by Elia Kazan, written by Budd Schulberg (Burbank, CA: Warner Bros., 1957).

15. I come to my understanding of Schulberg's non-allegiant politics through reading his letters, notes, and published writing archived at Dartmouth. In addition, I confirmed this perspective on Schulberg during conversations with Donna Myrow, who was his personal typist and who lived in his guest house during the WWW years, and with writer Robert Lipsyte, who was friends with Schulberg in the late 1960s and early 1970s (October 20, 2016; March 1, 2017, respectively).

16. See, for instance, Jerry Cohen and William S. Murphy, *Burn, Baby, Burn: The Los Angeles Race Riot, August 1965* (New York: Dutton, 1966).

17. Mike Davis, *City of Quartz: Excavating the Future in Los Angeles* (New York: Verso, 2006), 164.

18. Not that housing prices were cheap. Instead, with a densely concentrated population with limited options for moving elsewhere, landlords who lived outside of Watts could raise rents on a largely captive population. See David Harvey, *Social Justice and the City* (Athens: University of Georgia Press, 2009).

19. See Gaye Theresa Johnson, *Spaces of Conflict, Sounds of Solidarity: Music, Race, and Spatial Entitlement in Los Angeles* (Berkeley: University of California Press, 2013), 15.

20. According to Schulberg's assistant, Donna Myrow, prior to the establishment of Frederick Douglass House, Workshop writers would sometimes show up unannounced at Schulberg's own residence in Beverly Hills, much to the author's consternation. Myrow perceived Schulberg's frustration to be primarily about the encroachment on his own professional writing time, and not about the bidirectional dissolution of racial boundaries. In any case, it is noteworthy that Schulberg never writes about these visits, only about his own travels to Watts.

21. Daniel Widener's *Black Arts West* criticizes the Workshop as an example of dead-end liberalism, which subsumes an aesthetic project into a weak political agenda. In Widener's account, the black L.A. arts scene is divisible between radical and liberal arts projects, with liberalism ameliorating the more truly revolutionary potential at work in the Black Arts and Black Nationalist movements. Though Widener is overly dismissive of Schulberg as both an artist and an activist, he adequately captures how the Workshop was, without intention, absorbed into a largely liberal framework addressing poverty and race relations in the United States during the 1960s. Without a doubt, staffers in Congress and at the recently established National Foundation on the Arts and Humanities (as the governing body of the NEA and NEH was then called) considered the Workshop a showcase for integrationist, liberal messaging, and a safe bet for funding. However, contrary to Widener's claim that Schulberg was at home in the halls of Congress following his 1951 HUAC testimony, the Workshop had to continually lobby for national support, and Schulberg himself declined to speak to Congress when initially invited, accepting an invitation only when his writers Harry Dolan and Johnnie Scott were asked to come, the following year. Without wishing to claim that Schulberg's politics were not in fact liberal, and without disputing the liberal trajectory of the Workshop, I contend that beneath the phrasing of "liberal" and its companion "integrationist" we can locate a more complicated and at times contradictory set of circumstances, motivations, inclinations, and expectations at work in Schulberg's and others' development of the project. Rather than begin with the premise that Schulberg took Watts as a lab for his brand of liberalism, and the Workshop as his showcase and pet project, I begin with the assumption that Schulberg really did not understand what he had on hand in Watts during the first year, and that his Hollywood and Washington, D.C., fundraising efforts took on a (frustrating, time-sucking) life of their own.

Widener would put Schulberg in conflict with what he called "the young Angries" whose volatile spirit and nationalist politics and aesthetics often drowned out the nascent writing workshop at the Watts Happening Coffee House (Widener, *Black Arts West*, 97), but Schulberg clarified, "often I'd be asked if I were not afraid of the young angries of Watts and their successors whose hatred of whitey brought them to the brink of guerilla warfare. What I'm really afraid of are greed and selfishness and blind intransigence that build (yes, even 14 years after the revolt) concentration camp walls around enclaves like Watts" ("Seven Days That Shook Los Angeles," Budd Schulberg Collection, 1913–2014, the Rauner Special Collections Library at Dartmouth University, Box 22, Folder 21). Lines such as these suggest the perhaps nuanced, perhaps ambivalent stance of Schulberg toward Black Nationalist activists, for while he pins the animus on Black Nationalists, he implies that it is a justified hatred, sewn through both unintended and pointedly active efforts to sequester and suppress black lives—and this, the white oppression of black life rather than black hatred, is what we must combat.

22. James Baldwin, *No Name in the Street* (New York: Vintage, 2007), 124.

23. Henri Lefebvre, *The Production of Space*, trans. Donald Nicholson-Smith (Malden, MA: Blackwell, 1992), 313.

24. Ibid., 319.

25. Budd Schulberg Collection, Rauner manuscript MS-978, Box 106, Folder 20.

26. In the explanatory book published by the *Los Angeles Times* the year after the riots, the editors wrote, "many residents, when the riots broke out, had to consult maps to find out where Watts and Willowbrook were. They found out soon enough. By freeway, Watts was minutes away and there was a sudden sense of vulnerability and fear" (Cohen and Murphy, *Burn, Baby, Burn!*, 8).

27. Lefebvre, *The Production of Space*, 313.

28. Budd Schulberg Collection, Box 106, Folder 20.

29. Ibid.

30. Ibid.

31. Schulburg, *From the Ashes*, 19.

32. In his introduction to *From the Ashes*, Schulberg makes the unfavorable comparison between the prewar tenements of the Lower East Side in Manhattan and Watts, noting that Watts lacked the sort of neighborhood networks of parochial associations to support its residents. For a history of how the term *ghetto*, which was originally the space of Jewish sequestration in medieval Venice, came to signify black urban spaces of deprivation, see Mitchell Dunier, *Ghetto: The Invention of a Place, the History of an Idea* (New York: Farrar, Straus and Giroux, 2017).

33. Clover, *Riot, Strike, Riot.*

34. Manning Marable, *How Capitalism Underdeveloped Black America: Problems in Race, Political Economy, and Society* (Chicago: Haymarket, 2015).

35. Ibid.

36. Budd Schulberg Collection, Box 107, Folder 11.

37. Ibid., Box 107, Folder 9.

38. Donna Myrow told me an illustrative anecdote. Apparently, Schulberg held a garden-party fundraiser at his home in Beverly Hills, and near the end of the party, he made a speech and asked for contributions, whereupon his liberal friends shifted uncomfortably from foot to foot, while remaining silent. After some embarrassing and uncomfortable moments, the party's caterer, a successful black entrepreneur whom Schulberg had contracted on several prior occasions, stepped forward with checkbook in hand and announced that he was writing out a donation for one thousand dollars. Personal conversation, Oct 20, 2016.

39. Budd Schulberg Collection, Box 106, Folder 96.

40. *From the Ashes* closes with a peculiar set of appendices, documenting the arrest and trial of one of the Workshop writers, named "T" for privacy's sake. T was arrested in circumstances similar to the arrest of Marquette Frye, the driver

whose arrest sparked the Watts Riots two years before. The appendices document T's innocence, and Schulberg's dogged efforts to secure a public defender and character witnesses, including his own testimony. The section ends with an epilogue in which Schulberg writes of a riot averted, but rather than assume a salvational posture, or even suggest that it was better not to riot, he allows that of most importance is to write: the arrest, the defense, and the acquittal are enough to demonstrate the necessity of a writing community.

41. Budd Schulberg Collection, Box 106, Folder 61.

42. Ibid., Box 106, Folder 14.

43. See Emmanuel Levinas, "Peace and Proximity," in *Basic Philosophical Writings*, ed. Adriaan T. Peperzak, Simon Critchley, and Robert Bernasconi (Bloomington: Indiana University Press, 1996).

44. See Hannah Arendt, *Love and Saint Augustine*, ed. Joanna Vecchiarelli Scott and Judith Chelius Stark (Chicago: University of Chicago Press, 1998).

45. "Dialog in Black and White," *Playboy* 13, no. 12, December 1966. The conversation occurred in several locations across several months, and though redacted into a tight exchange for publication, the unpublished transcripts, including Schulberg's emendations, are thrilling for the way they range far beyond any simple ideologies or categories of identity. I cite from the published version when possible, and the transcripts for those exchanges that did not make it into print.

46. Budd Schulberg Collection, Box 106, Folder 10.

47. "Dialog in Black and White," 281.

48. Budd Schulberg Collection, Box 106, Folder 10.

49. Ibid.

50. Ibid., Box 6, Folder 10.

51. Ibid.

52. Ibid., Box 106, Folder 10.

53. George Shulman, *American Prophecy: Race and Redemption in American Political Culture* (Minneapolis: University of Minnesota Press, 2008.

54. "Dialog in Black and White," 282, 286.

55. Budd Schulberg Collection, Box 106, Folder 11, page 21 of typed manuscript.

56. James Baldwin, *The Fire Next Time* (New York: Vintage, 1993), 109.

57. Talmadge Spratt, "About the Douglass House Foundation," *Negro American Literature Forum* 4.3 (Autumn 1970): 76.

58. Ibid.

59. Paul Beatty, *The Sellout* (New York: Farrar, Straus and Giroux, 2015).

60. "Straight Outta Compton . . . On Horseback," *All Things Considered*, National Public Radio, April 3, 2011, http://www.npr.org/2011/04/03/134981907/straight-outta-compton-on-horseback.

61. Ben Schott, "Solastalgia," "Schott's Vocab: A Miscellany of Modern Words and Phrases," *The New York Times*, May 17, 2011, https://schott.blogs.nytimes.com /2011/05/17/solastalgia.

62. Moten, "Blackness and Nothingness," 778.

63. Chris Jackson, "Our Thing: An Interview with Paul Beatty," *The Paris Review*, May 7, 2015, https://www.theparisreview.org/blog/2015/05/07/our-thing -an-interview-with-paul-beatty.

64. "'Community' in Los Angeles means homogeneity of race, class, and especially home values. Community designations [in Los Angeles . . .] have no legal status. In the last analysis, they are merely favors granted by city council members to well-organized neighborhoods or businessmen's groups seeking to have their areas identified" (Davis, City of Quartz, 153).

65. Judith Madera, *Black Atlas: Geography and Flow in Nineteenth Century African American Literature* (Durham, NC: Duke University Press, 2015), 5.

66. See Cheryl Harris, "Whiteness as Property," *Harvard Law Review* 106, no. 8 (June 1993), https://doi.org/10.2307/1341787.

67. Baldwin, *Fire Next Time*, 102.

68. Moten, "Blackness and Nothingness," 749.

CHAPTER 3: My Neighborhood

1. Henri Lefebvre, *The Production of Space*, trans. Donald Nicholson-Smith (Malden, MA: Blackwell, 1992), 6.

2. Sigmund Freud, *Civilization and Its Discontents* (New York: Norton, 2010).

3. Emmanuel Levinas, "Peace and Proximity," in *Basic Philosophical Writings*, ed. Adriaan T. Peperzak, Simon Critchley, and Robert Bernasconi (Bloomington: Indiana University Press, 1996), 165, 167.

4. I am aware that Rancière is caustically dismissive of ethics, especially as sourced in Levinas. I am sympathetic to his critique of an overly eager resolution of ethics in various modes of recognition, including normative human rights law and policy, and I share his dismissal of a quietist politics that assigns the field of politics to the ruling powers of what he calls "police"—politics as the maintenance of the usual. Still, despite how he has been appropriated, Levinas himself makes no accommodation of his ethics to politics.

5. Slavoj Žižek, "Smashing the Neighbor's Face," Lacan Dotcom, 1997/2005, http://www.lacan.com/zizsmash.htm; Thomas Claviez, "A Metonymic Community? Toward a Poetics of Contingency," in *The Common Growl: Toward a Poetics of Precarious Community* (New York: Fordham University Press, 2016).

6. Gilles Deleuze and Felix Guattari, *A Thousand Plateaus: Capitalism and Schizophrenia*, trans. Brian Massumi (Minneapolis: Minnesota University Press, 1987).

7. Adam Zachary Newton, *Facing Black and Jew: Literature as Public Space in Twentieth-Century America* (New York: Cambridge University Press, 1999), 12.

8. Ibid.

9. See Ernesto Laclau, *The Rhetorical Foundations of Society* (New York: Verso, 2014).

10. See Fred Moten, "Blackness and Nothingness (Mysticism in the Flesh)," *The South Atlantic Quarterly* 112, no. 4 (Fall 2013).

11. Edward W. Soja, *Postmodern Geographies: The Reassertion of Space in Critical Social Theory* (New York: Verso, 1989), 190.

12. Ibid., 223.

13. Ibid., 151.

14. Michel de Certeau, *The Practice of Everyday Life*, trans. Steven F. Rendall (Berkeley: University of California Press, 2011), 178.

15. See Denis Wood, *Rethinking the Power of Maps* (New York: Guilford, 2010); Alexis Bhagat and Lize Mogel, "Introduction," in *An Atlas of Radical Cartography*, ed. Lize Mogel and Alexis Bhagat (Los Angeles: Journal of Aesthetics and Protest Press, 2008).

16. Charlotte Elisheva Fonrobert, "The Political Symbolism of the Eruv," *Jewish Social Studies* 11, no. 3 (Spring/Summer 2005): 22, https://doi.org/10.1353/jss.2005.0023.

17. Ibid., 28.

18. An image posted on the website for the L.A. Eruv features a photo apparently taken at a ceremony for renting the eruv area. In the photo, Jewish leaders and the sheriff hold up a note of agreement. The note reads, "As a member of the Jewish community of Los Angeles, on behalf of all the members of the Jewish Community of Los Angeles County, I would like to rent *the area* within your jurisdiction as Sheriff of Los Angeles County for a period of 20 years, beginning today . . . for the total sum of one dollar in order to incorporate this area for the purpose of Eruv." Image accessed August 31, 2017, http://www.laeruv.com/eruv-guide/permission-from-los-angeles.

19. Soja, *Postmodern Geographies*, 153.

20. Zachary Heiden, "Fences and Neighbors," *Law and Literature* 17, no. 2 (Summer 2005): 228, https://doi.org/10.1525/lal.2005.17.2.225.

21. Alexandra Lang Sussman, "Strings Attached: An Analysis of the Eruv Under the Religion Clauses of the First Amendment and the Religious Land Use and Institutionalized Persons Act," *The University of Maryland Law Journal of Race, Religion, Gender & Class* 9, no. 1 (Spring 2009): 95.

22. Manuel Herz, "Institutionalized Experiment: The Politics of 'Jewish Architecture' in Germany," *Jewish Social Studies* 11, no. 3 (Spring/Summer 2005): 59, https://doi.org/10.1353/jss.2005.0024.

23. Lefebvre, *The Production of Space*, 59.

24. Though outside the scope of this study, Michael Chabon's novel *The Yiddish Policeman's Union* explores exactly this phenomenal linking of speculative and material worlds, imagining a sanctuary for Jewish Holocaust refugees in Sitka, Alaska, which thrives for three generations as a nation-within-the-nation, but is fated to disappear when, according to a law of "reversion," the original U.S. legislation establishing the refuge expires. Notably, the novel's plot runs through a shaggy-dog storyline involving the "boundary maven," or local boss of Sitka's eruv. See Michael Chabon, *The Yiddish Policeman's Union* (New York: HarperCollins, 2007).

25. *OED Online*, s.v. "area (n.)," accessed Sept 1, 2017, http://www.oed.com /view/Entry/10505?redirectedFrom=area#eid.

26. See Michael Warner, *Publics and Counterpublics* (New York: Zone Books, 2005).

27. Cheryl Harris, "Whiteness as Property," *Harvard Law Review* 106, no. 8 (June 1993), https://doi.org/10.2307/1341787.

28. Ibid., 1721.

29. Ibid.

30. Mark Wild, *Street Meeting: Multiethnic Neighborhoods in Early Twentieth-Century Los Angeles* (Berkeley: University of California Press, 2008), 38.

31. Fonrobert, "Political Symbolism of the Eruv," 24.

32. Ibid., 6.

33. Ibid., 29.

34. Bruce Stokes, "Are American Jews Turning Away from Israel?," *Foreign Policy*, March 10, 2016, http://foreignpolicy.com/2016/03/10/are-american-jews -turning-away-from-israel/?utm_source=Sailthru&utm_medium=email&utm _campaign=New%20Campaign&utm_term=Flashpoints.

35. Janine Rayford, "Freedom Within Bounds: Inside L.A.'s Eruv Communities," *Neon Tommy*, Annenberg Media Center, University of Southern California, January 15, 2011, http://www.neontommy.com/news/2011/02/freedom-within -bounds-inside-la-s-eruv-communities.

36. Leah Mirakhor, "After the Revolution to the War on Terror: Iranian Jewish American Literature in the United States," *Studies in American Jewish Literature* 35.1 (2016): 33–51.

37. See David Nirenberg, "'Judaism' as Political Concept: Toward a Critique of Political Theology," *Representations* 128, no. 1 (Fall 2014), https://doi.org/10.1525 /rep.2014.128.1.1.

38. See Ranen Omer-Sherman, *Diaspora and Zionism in Jewish American Literature: Lazarus, Syrkin, Reznikoff, and Roth* (Waltham, MA: Brandeis University Press, 2002).

39. David Friedman, "Read Peter Beinart and You'll Vote Donald Trump,"

Arutz Sheva, June 5, 2016, http://www.israelnationalnews.com/Articles/Article.
aspx/18828; also Matthew Rosenberg, "Trump Chooses Hard-Liner as Ambassador to Israel," *New York Times*, December 15, 2016, https://www.nytimes
.com/2016/12/15/us/politics/donald-trump-david-friedman-israel-ambassador.html
?smid=tw-bna&_r=0.

40. Ryan Torok, "L.A. Rabbis Arrested at ICE Protest," *Jewish Journal*, April 13,
2017, http://jewishjournal.com/news/los_angeles/217897/ice-protest-l-leads-arrests.

41. Judith Butler, *Parting Ways: Jewishness and the Critique of Zionism* (New
York: Columbia University Press, 2012), 3.

42. Ibid., 15.

43. Ibid., 19.

44. Edward W. Said, *Freud and the Non-European* (New York: Verso, 2003).

45. See Butler, *Parting Ways*, chap. 1, "Impossible, Necessary Task: Said, Levinas, and the Ethical Demand," 28–53.

46. Butler, *Parting Ways*, 166.

47. See William E. Connolly, *Pluralism* (Durham, NC: Duke University
Press, 2005).

48. Butler, *Parting Ways*, 127.

49. *My Neighbourhood*, directed by Julia Bacha and Rebekah Wingert-Jabi, Just
Vision, Accessed February 16, 2018, https://www.justvision.org/myneighbourhood
/watch.

50. Jaclynn Ashly, "Sheikh Jarrah: When My Enemy Is My Neighbor," *Al
Jazeera*, October 3, 2016, http://www.aljazeera.com/news/2016/09/sheikh-jarrah
-enemy-neighbour-160905093721434.html.

51. Ibid.

52. Butler, *Parting Ways*, 53.

53. "Our Mural: 'A Shenere Un Besere Velt' (A More Beautiful and Better
World)," SoCal Arbeter Ring/Workmen's Circle, accessed August 15, 2017, http://
circlesocal.org/about/mural.

54. Kevin Stricke, "Workmen's Circle Mural: A More Beautiful and Better World in South Robertson," *KCET*, January 9, 2014, https://www.kcet.org/
shows/departures/workmens-circle-mural-a-more-beautiful-and-better-world
-in-south-robertson.

55. Ryan Torok, "Painting Love Over Hate on Vandalized Workmen's Circle Mural," *Jewish Journal*, March 19, 2014, http://jewishjournal.com/news/los
_angeles/127793.

56. Lefebvre, *The Production of Space*, 73.

57. Jean-Luc Nancy, "Foreword: The Common Growl," in *The Common
Growl: Toward a Poetics of Precarious Community*, ed. Thomas Claviez (New York:
Fordham University Press, 2016), ix.

58. Ibid.

CONCLUSION: Love, Space, and
the Grounds of Comparative Ethnic Literature Study

1. Bruno Latour, *Reassembling the Social: An Introduction to Actor-Network Theory* (Oxford, UK: Oxford University Press, 2005), 35.

2. See, for instance, "Photographers Becoming Security Concerns," *Morning Edition*, National Public Radio, June 16, 2005, http://www.npr.org/templates /story/story.php?storyId=4705698.

3. Guy Ernest Debord, "Theory of the Derive," Situationist Central Texts, Department of Art-Locative Media Territories Winter 2006 Course, UCSB, August 15, 2017, http://www.arts.ucsb.edu/classes/ART22W06/situtexts.html.

4. See, for instance, Arte Público's series, "Recovering the U.S. Hispanic Literary Heritage; Raúl Coronado, *A World Not to Come: A History of Latino Writing and Print Culture* (Cambridge, MA: Harvard University Press, 2013); Rodrigo Lazo and Jesse Alemán, *The Latino Nineteenth Century: Archival Encounters in American Literary History* (New York: New York University Press, 2016); María Josefina Saldaña-Portillo, *Indian Given: Racial Geographies Across Mexico and the United States* (Durham, NC: Duke University Press, 2016); María Josefina Saldaña-Portillo, *The Revolutionary Imagination in the Americas and the Age of Development* (Durham, NC: Duke University Press, 2003); Paula M. L. Moya and Ramon Saldivar, "Fictions of the Trans-American Imaginary," *MFS Modern Fiction Studies* 49, no. 1 (Spring 2013), https://doi.org/10.1353/mfs.2003.0007.

5. The exceptions are Jonathan Boyarin's *The Unconverted Self: Jews, Indians, and the Identity of Christian Europe* (Chicago: University of Chicago Press, 2009) and Sarah Casteel Phillips's *Calypso Jews: Jewishness in the Caribbean Literary Imagination* (New York: Columbia University Press, 2016).

6. See Dean Franco, *Race, Rights, and Recognition: Jewish American Literature Since 1969* (Ithaca, NY: Cornell University Press, 2012).

7. See Gaye Theresa Johnson, *Spaces of Conflict, Sounds of Solidarity: Music, Race, and Spatial Entitlement in Los Angeles* (Berkeley: University of California Press, 2013).

8. See Christopher Douglas, *A Genealogy of Literary Multiculturalism* (Ithaca, NY: Cornell University Press, 2009).

9. Vilna Bashi Treitler, *The Ethnic Project: Transforming Racial Fiction into Ethnic Factions* (Stanford, CA: Stanford University Press, 2013), 97.

10. See Aamir R. Mufti, *Enlightenment in the Colony: The Jewish Question and the Crisis of Postcolonial Culture* (Princeton, NJ: Princeton University Press, 2007); Bryan Cheyette, *Diasporas of the Mind: Jewish and Postcolonial Writing and the Nightmare of History* (New Haven, CT: Yale University Press, 2014); Jonathan Freedman, *Klezmer America: Jewishness, Ethnicity, Modernity* (New York: Columbia University Press, 2009); Rachel Rubinstein, *Members of the Tribe: Native America in the Jewish Imagination* (Detroit: Wayne State University Press, 2010); Eric

Sundquist, *Strangers in the Land: Blacks, Jews, Post-Holocaust America* (Cambridge, MA: Harvard University Press, 2009); Josh Lambert, *Unclean Lips: Obscenity, Jews, and American Culture* (New York: New York University Press, 2013); Benjamin Schreier, *The Impossible Jew: Identity and the Reconstruction of Jewish American Literary History* (New York: New York University Press, 2015).

11. Robert Alter, "What Jewish Studies Can Do," *Commentary*, October 1, 1974, https://www.commentarymagazine.com/articles/what-jewish-studies-can-do.

12. See Susannah Heschel, "Jewish Studies as Counterhistory," in *Insider/Outsider: American Jews and Multiculturalism*, ed. David Biale, Michael Galchinksy, and Susannah Heschel (Berkeley: University of California Press, 1998).

13. Johnson, *Spaces of Conflict*, 78.

14. Schreier, *The Impossible Jew*.

15. Barbara Mann, *Space and Place in Jewish Studies* (New Brunswick, NJ: Rutgers University Press, 2011), 130–131.

16. See, for instance, the defense of Barrio Logan in San Diego, which is Chicanx -identified similar to Boyle Heights. In a 2017 clash between alt-right agitators and Barrio Logan defenders, one Latina, Tania Marquez, explained, "This is who we are as Latinos," gesturing to the park around her. "It talks about the struggles of the people through the years. It's identified as a place of community, of coming together, and knowing your roots. It has great significance." See Lyndsay Winkley, "Far-Right Activists and Counter-Protesters Clash at Chicano Park in San Diego," *Los Angeles Times*, September 4, 2017, http://www.latimes.com/local/lanow/la-me-chicano-park-protest-20170904-story.html.

17. See Dean Franco, "Pluralism and Postmodernism: The Histories and Geographies of Ethnic American Literature," in *The Cambridge Companion to Postmodern American Fiction*, ed. Paula Geyh (Cambridge, UK: Cambridge University Press, 2017).

18. See Amy Hungerford, *Postmodern Belief: American Literature and Religion Since 1960* (Princeton, NJ: Princeton University Press, 2010).

19. Fred Moten's work is marked by an engagement with Derrida, among other poststructuralists. Here's how Moten put it in an interview: "So, that's what *In the Break* is about—I'm not trying to *use* or *apply* Marx and Freud and Derrida and Lacan or whoever—I'm interested in their work, not even so much because I think it helps to illuminate something elsewhere, but I feel like in the rubbing together, in the haptic sort of rub that exists independently of my kind of bringing them together, there's something that exists between Freud and Baraka, between Freud and DuBois, between Derrida and Adrian Piper, even though she might not like him, and that rub, that hapticality, is what I'm invested in, and if I was to put it in a simple kind of way I would say that the way I read Freud and Marx is that they are a part of the black radical tradition. And I read them that way, rather than trying to create a kind of text that kind of makes an argument for Baraka being a full-fledged,

vested member of the Western intellectual and aesthetic canon." See Fred Moten, "An Interview with Fred Moten, Pt. II: On Radical Indistinctness and Thought Flavor à la Derrida," interview by Adam Fitzgerald, *Literary Hub*, August 6, 2015, http://lithub.com/an-interview-with-fred-moten-pt-ii. See also Homi K. Bhabha, *The Location of Culture*, 2nd ed. (New York: Routledge, 2005); Gayatri Chakravorty Spivak, *A Critique of Postcolonial Reason: Toward a History of the Vanishing Present* (Cambridge, MA.: Harvard University Press, 1999); Ian Baucom, *Specters of the Atlantic: Finance Capital, Slavery, and the Philosophy of History* (Durham, NC: Duke University Press, 2005). On Derrida's interest in race, Herman Rapaport is currently working on Derrida's late archives at Irvine and reports that Derrida was thinking about race and identity repeatedly in his final lectures (personal conversation, March 2016). But the interest in race has been present for decades. "Certainly 'Auschwitz' as you [Richard Rand] correctly state has never been 'very far from my thoughts.' It would be easy to show this, though I have no wish to do so. The thought of the incineration of the holocaust, of cinders, runs through all my texts, well before *Of Spirit* which speaks exclusively of this, and well before *Cinders* which includes the necessary references. . . . *Auschwitz has obsessed everything that I have ever been able to think.*" Richard Rand, ed., *Logomachia: The Conflict of the Faculties Today.* (Nebraska, 1992), 211, emphasis added. My thanks to Herman Rapaport for a fruitful discussion on Derrida and for the citation.

20. Hungerford, *Postmodern Belief,* xx.

21. See Ana Castillo, *So Far From God* (New York: W.W. Norton, 2005); Tomás Rivera, . . . *And the Earth Did Not Devour Him,* trans. Evangelina Vigil-Piñón (St. Louis: Turtleback Books, 2015); Alejandro Morales, *The Rag Doll Plagues* (Houston: Arte Público Press, 1992); Sandra Cisneros, *Woman Hollering Creek and Other Stories* (New York: Vintage, 1992).

22. Bernard Malamud, "Angel Levine," *The Magic Barrel: Stories,* rep. ed. (New York: Farrar, Straus and Giroux, 2003), 55.

23. The hermetic character of Malamud's story typically directs critics toward its moral or universal theme, and rarely does anyone discuss the particular details of space and race in the story, that Manischevitz has to make his way from the Lower East Side to Harlem, a place both menacing and familiar, and the grounds of his choice to believe. This may be why Budd Schulberg, who was friends with Malamud, sought his views on a manuscript he had written about race and the spectacle of boxing, recognizing that though Malamud's style was vastly different from his own, both writers thought about both moral injustice and material inequity. I know about Schulberg's letter to Malamud because Josh Lambert discovered it while researching in Malamud's archives. I am grateful to Josh for sharing it with me, unbidden.

INDEX

Page numbers in italics refer to images; those followed by n refer to notes, with note number.

The Fire Next Time (Baldwin), 97, 107
Fonrobert, Charlotte, 125, 132–33
The Forward, 147
Foucault, Michel, 68, 127
Frederick Douglass House: burning of,
    by FBI informant, 77, 98; destruc-
    tion of, as end of brief cultural re-
    naissance, 77; founding of, 29, 77;
    leasing and remodeling of property
    for, 88; limited longterm impact
    of, 77; as metaphor of metonymy,
    98–99; reasons for founding, 84,
    86–87; Schulberg on importance
    of, 78; Schulberg's difficulty fund-
    ing, 87, 184n38; success of, 77;
    users' conflicting demands on, 98
freedom: for all, impossibility of, when
    freedom derives from identity, 95;
    literature as means of imaging, 60
freeways: as barriers, in Beatty's *The
    Sellout*, 107–8; as border, in Vira-
    montes's *Their Dogs Came with
    Them*, 40; as both border and line,
    25, 101, 175–76n40; as connection
    and division, 6–7; cordoning off of
    Watts by, 79, 80–81; as opportunity
    afforded to white residents at ex-
    pense of others, 73–74; as segregat-
    ing barriers, 79, 181n7; as target of
    rioters, 74, 181n8; as violent nega-
    tion of other, 81
Freud, Sigmund, 51, 114, 115, 140, 191n19
Freud and the Non-European (Said),
    140–41
Friedman, David, 134, 136
From the Ashes: Voices of Watts (Watts
    Writers Workshop): appendices on
    arrest and trial of "T," 183–84n38;
    Schulberg's introduction to, 82–83,
    183n32; as Watts Writers Workshop
    anthology, 76; works on oppressive
    conditions in Watts, 84–86
Fry, Marquette, 183–84n38

Gates, Henry Louis, Jr., 163
Gehry, Frank, 167–68
Genealogy of Literary Multiculturalism
    (Douglas), 160

gentrification: balanced political re-
    sponses to injustices of, 61–62; in
    Boyle Heights, 158, 180n58; in East
    Los Angeles, 158
Gold, Jonathan, 1–2
Gordon, Eric, 148–49
Grandison, K. Ian, 175–76n40, 181n7
grandparents of author: courtship and
    marriage, 156–57; ethnic back-
    ground of, 2, 156–57; grandfather's
    surly temper, 157; home in Pico-
    Robertson district, 2; intermar-
    riage, problems caused by, 2;
    unplanned visit to former home of,
    156–57
Gray, Freddie, 71–72
Gregory, Dick, 90
Grosz, Elizabeth, 54
Guattari, Felix, 24, 50

Hames-García, Michael, 13–14, 17, 138
Harpers magazine, 84
Harris, Cheryl, 131–32
Harvard Law Review, 131
Hayot, Eric, 179n50
hegemonic identification, 7–8
hegemony, metaphorical and met-
    onymical identity in, 16–17
Heiden, Zachary, 127
Herz, Manuel, 129
Highland Avenue, Los Angeles, busi-
    nesses and attractions on, 120
Hillel, controversy over Israeli policies
    in, 136
Himes, Chester, 11
Hollywood Freeway (101), as connec-
    tion and division, 6–7
homeless persons in L.A., 153–54
Honig, Bonnie, 58–59
"The House on Mettler Street" (Tay-
    lor), 85, 86
Hsu, Hsuan, 44, 45
humanities, on race as product of lan-
    guage, 5
Hungerford, Amy, 168–69
Husserl, Edmund, 18

identitarian credentials of author, 2–3
identification: as doorway to metaphor,

200

Stanford Studies in
COMPARATIVE RACE AND ETHNICITY

Published in collaboration with the Center for Comparative Studies
in Race and Ethnicity, Stanford University

SERIES EDITORS
Hazel Rose Markus
Paula M. L. Moya

Black Power and Palestine: Transnational Countries of Color
Michael R. Fischbach
2019

*Race and Upward Mobility: Seeking, Gatekeeping,
and Other Class Strategies in Postwar America*
Elda María Román
2017

*The Emotional Politics of Racism: How Feelings
Trump Facts in an Era of Colorblindness*
Paula Ioanide
2015

*Beneath the Surface of White Supremacy:
Denaturalizing U.S. Racisms Past and Present*
Moon-Kie Jung
2015